LOST
MYRTLE BEACH

BECKY BILLINGSLEY

Charleston   London

THE
History
PRESS

Published by The History Press
Charleston, SC 29403
www.historypress.net

Back cover, middle inset: Ferris wheel at night. *Author's collection.*

First published 2014

Manufactured in the United States

ISBN 978.1.62619.392.5

Library of Congress CIP data applied for.

CONTENTS

FOREWORD

When we look at Myrtle Beach today, we see all the lifestyles—from relaxed retirees to busy hospitality worker bees—and the entertainment going on, and we plan our activities around them. However, it is important to look at happenings from years ago that were overlooked, lost or changed that influence what we see today.

We lost great landscapes and views to development with the clear-cutting of dense forests and beachfront properties' verdure to make way for magnificent hotels and homes. These are required for living and visiting here, but they took the place of older and architecturally significant beach homes and businesses.

Some of these were well-constructed, well-kept and comfortable buildings for hardy souls who moved here and embraced the beach lifestyle in their personal lives and businesses. They preserved the lush, natural landscapes that were here for previous generations. We had forests of yaupon holly, wax myrtles, longleaf pines, natural magnolia growths, sea grasses and hickories, but they were replaced by imported palms of many types that are now in their northernmost ranges and don't provide lush, shady spots. We cannot see around, over or through the oceanfront development to enjoy a wide view of the ocean.

Most of the fabulous places of the earlier years were not preserved for their architecture and history.

We recall the Seaside Inn, which was built on a walkway to the beach. It was situated far back from the oceanfront, so as to be useful and compatible to many families for many years, before being moved. The Ocean Forest area was also built back from the beach so all who were there could enjoy the view and relax in an area of beautifully maintained natural growth. There again a planned and maintained architecture was built for local beauty, not an imported style.

The whole downtown area around Seventh and Eighth Avenues North was anchored by the Flatiron Building, and across the street was the widely recognized and loved Myrtle Beach Pavilion, where visitors always went on their first day at Myrtle Beach. Both are gone.

Our beach uses have been changed and curtailed by local businesses and lines of use, which do not allow free and comfortable access to the ocean for families and children. Hotels or beach services set out lines of chairs and umbrellas and are quick to tell people who bring their own beach gear where they may or may not sit down. This is not the spirit of public beach access.

Does anyone remember driving on the beach at low tide in your Jeep or on your sand sail boat? Do you recall a secret walk on the beach at 2:00 a.m. after parking at a tree-covered spot? Or walking on the beach as you heard the sounds of the Kay Kaiser band playing on the moonlit terrace at the Ocean Forest? And do you recall skinny-dipping in the ocean after midnight?

I hope that remembering what is lost will inspire people to speak up and let city leaders know we want our past preserved and our beaches in natural states before even more of our heritage is forever lost.

BARBARA WARD HORNER
News Archivist at the Sun News
1987–2008

ACKNOWLEDGEMENTS

Myrtle Beach natives love where they grew up, and millions of annual visitors return each year for traditional family vacations. They may not be overjoyed with summer traffic snarls, but people feel strong affinities for the ocean and beaches, forests, rivers, seafood, parties, nightlife, concerts, theater shows, motorcycle rallies, miniature golf, amusement parks, fishing, parasailing, banner planes, restaurants, beach stores and the rest of the vibrant spectacle for which Myrtle Beach is known.

Thank you to those who kindly shared their experiences regarding Myrtle Beach's colorful history. You gave honest answers to earnest questions, and perhaps those answers will help preserve other pieces of your heritage. Many local residents contributed interviews and photos, and you will meet them as you read *Lost Myrtle Beach*. As much as possible their recollections are documented in their own words.

Specific thanks go to:

Barbara Horner, who presented me with a shoebox full of *Sun News* history column clippings she diligently saved during the twenty years she was the newspaper's archivist. It was a pleasure to read them and reference those historians' work. She also shared a lifetime of coastal reminiscences.

Transcriptionist and researcher David Schwartz, who helped this project meet a tight deadline. It was handy having a son, Adam Billingsley, who worked at Hard Rock Park and Freestyle Music Park and could edit and enhance that section.

ACKNOWLEDGEMENTS

Jack Bourne, a local historian and photo archivist who showed me photos and filled in many gaps. Jack introduced me to his mom and stepdad (Ed and Joyce Herian), and they explained the past with vivid, entertaining stories while we munched Joyce's excellent snickerdoodles.

Marion Haynes at the Horry County Museum, who was extremely helpful by pointing me to delightful vintage images.

Horry County Board of Architectural Review charter member and local architect Joel Carter, city of Myrtle Beach Planning director Jack Walker and senior planner Diane Moskow-McKenzie, who provided invaluable insight into the work that remains to be done to ensure Myrtle Beach's historic properties remain for future generations to enjoy and appreciate. The key, they say, is to speak up!

INTRODUCTION

The history of Myrtle Beach is a joyous, tumultuous and wildly interesting story. As of 2014, it has been an incorporated city for seventy-six years, but Myrtle Beach's unique geography helped its residents pack what would normally be a few centuries' worth of living into a much tighter timespan.

New traditions will be made, but this is a chronicle of what has been lost. These are the voices and opinions of locals and visitors from the previous three hundred years that have been collected so they, too, are not lost.

Locals interviewed for this book feel extreme sadness for some of Myrtle Beach's lost places and traditions. They understand the world moves on and they can't live in a time capsule, but many want to see more of the city's past preserved.

It is to be expected that a tourist area like Myrtle Beach would tear down old structures to make room for new and bigger ones that can house the millions of visitors who come each year, but some that are gone leave sore spots in the hearts of those who loved them. The Chesterfield Inn, the Ocean Forest Hotel and the Myrtle Beach Pavilion are places of particular note that are missed. The Sun Fun Festival isn't a place, but those who enjoyed it for sixty years cherished the celebrities and parade and cheerful beach games.

Restaurants, bars and nightclubs are not mentioned much because my editor and I decided that so many of those businesses have opened and closed in Myrtle Beach they deserve their own book. There also wasn't room to talk about every single landmark and amusement that has come and gone (the number of them is staggering considering Myrtle Beach's brief history!), but significant ones are here with information about them that even natives may not have heard before now. Memories that didn't fit into the book can be found in blog entries at beckybillingsley.com.

1

ISOLATED BEAUTY

Four hundred years ago, the Myrtle Beach area was not developed, but it had residents. The gorgeous wide beach, which is part of a large curving piece of coastline called Long Bay, was surrounded and isolated by forests, swamps, Carolina bays and rivers on three sides and the Atlantic Ocean on the east. Native Americans lived in the maritime forests.

Some of those Indians—called collectively Siouans, due to their commonality of language—had year-round camps near the coast and along tidal rivers. Others migrated to the beach with seasonal seafood rhythms. Buffalo roamed the coastal plains and were an important food source.

By the early sixteenth century, the heyday of local Native Americans was over due to the arrival of Europeans, who brought diseases such as smallpox, measles and influenza for which Native Americans had no resistance. By the mid-1700s, their numbers greatly reduced by illness, Native Americans were forced away from their lands and scattered, and some were enslaved. A tiny percentage remains today, including members of the Chicora tribe and the state-recognized Waccamaw Indian People, but they have lost the choice to live their lives as their ancestors did before Europeans came.

Since the Indians were moved from their ancestral lands, learning about their lives is difficult. They didn't have a written language, so most historic observation is through studying their tools and pottery shards found in campsites, such as around remnants of shellfish piles, called middens, which are curiously dense with clamshells instead of oyster shells at the south end of the Grand Strand.

"It's sad that we don't know more about our Native American culture," local historian Lee Brockington said. "That loss of handing down from generation to generation—we would have known about the shell middens if [the Indians] hadn't been removed from their land."

Although European settlers edged out the native inhabitants in the eighteenth century, the piece of coastline surrounding present-day Myrtle Beach remained isolated for generations and, therefore, was known as the Independent Republic. As area plantations utilized slave labor and the number of African Americans reached 90 percent of the South Carolina population in 1740, whites devised a plan to increase the number of white settlers. "Alarmed by the burgeoning slave population," as noted in the 2009 Horry County Historic Resources Survey, "the first royal governor of South Carolina, Robert Johnson, proposed a settlement plan for the frontier of the colony in 1730, hoping to attract white colonists. He offered incentives such as 50 acres of land for each family member, and funds for tools, transportation, and food with quit rents waived for 10 years."

Slowly, settlers moved in to farm, fish and make turpentine and tar from the pine trees. The beach was nice for seafood harvests and cooling swims during summer's steamy heat, but the land itself was considered practically worthless because it was too sandy for farming. Myrtle Beach, which didn't even have a name back then, has no deep port. Consequently, big vessels couldn't dock there as they did in Georgetown to the south and Little River to the north.

Its surrounding swampy geography made getting to the area that is now the heart of Myrtle Beach, in the middle of Long Bay, too much trouble for most beach visitors prior to 1900. A 1757 map doesn't show any named landmarks for miles around present-day Myrtle Beach, while a 1775 map depicts Lewis Swash at the present-day Singleton Swash. Robert Mills's 1825 atlas of the state of South Carolina shows a huge area to the west inscribed with the ominous name "Impassable Bay."

In 1784, a German traveler named Johann David Schoepf recorded his journey along the South Carolina coast, and his first stop was at Jeremiah Vareen's tavern that was just south of present-day North Myrtle Beach. While at Vareen's he saw "the skin of a female red tiger or cougar (*Felis concolor Linn*), which had been brought down in the neighborhood a few days before…The man who killed it came almost upon it in the woods, before he observed it; it fled before him from tree to tree, until he could bring it down with his gun." After leaving the tavern, Schoepf said his next stop to

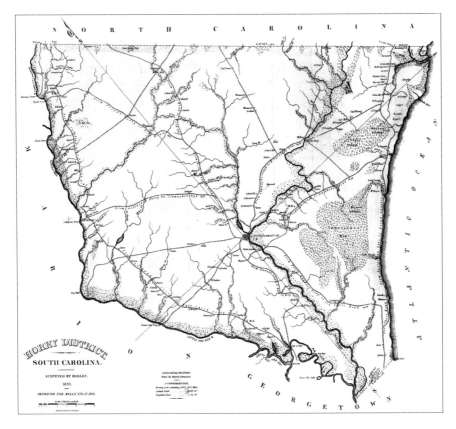

This 1825 Robert Mills map shows an "Impassable Bay" west of Myrtle Beach. *Author's collection.*

the south "before reaching the next human habitation" was an expanse of twenty-six miles:

> *Proceeding from the last-named plantation, after a few miles of woods-road, one comes to the so-called Long Bay or Beach. Here for 16 miles the common highway runs very near the shore. Lonely and desolate as this part of the road is, without shade and with no dwellings in sight, it is by no means a tedious road. The number of shells washed up, sponges, corals, sea-grasses and weeds, medusa, and many other ocean-products which strew the beach, engage and excite the attention of the traveller at every step... This beach-road consisted for the most part of shell-sand, coarse or fine, with very few, often no quartz-grains. So far as the otherwise loose sand is moistened by the play of the waves it forms an extremely smooth*

and firm surface, hardly showing hoof-marks. At a distance of perhaps 30-50 paces from the water, there runs parallel with it a line of low sand-swells, 3-6 ft. high and averaging 8-1-ft. across. Towards the sea these undulations were cut away almost perpendicularly, but on the other side were sloping and sparsely grown up with thin grass and bush. Those sand-swells which the ocean itself seems to have set as its limit, were notwithstanding broken through here and there, and the land lying immediately behind was much ravaged as a result of occasional overflow. The road leaving the beach, which extends far away of a similar character, one again traverses gloomy and lonesome woods to the neighborhood of the Waccama or Waggomangh, and beyond, by a narrow tongue of land between that river and the ocean, to Winguah Bay.

In 1801 the area around Long Bay finally had an official name: Horry, named after Revolutionary War hero Brigadier General Peter Horry (1747–1815). "By 1810," the 2009 historic property survey says, "Horry had a total population of 4,348; it was the lowest in the state by over 600 people, with 1,398 enslaved individuals, and 18 free people of color...In another decade, Horry had little growth, only reaching 5,025 people in 1820, again the lowest in the state, and by an even wider margin of 1,400 people."

By 1840, the Horry district had 5,750 residents, but the area around Myrtle Beach wasn't yet populated enough to have a post office. The 1850 census counted 7,646 residents and 731 farms, and ten years later, in 1860, the number of residents was 7,962. The coastline shown in an 1856 map shows Lewis Swash, Eight Mile Swash and a third unnamed swash that was likely Withers Swash. By 1870, the Horry district had become Horry County, and its population was more than 10,000.

Starting in 1900, when the first train came to Myrtle Beach, the area's deforestation began in earnest. The train that brought tourists to the area carried away its lumber.

FERRIES

Horry County is pockmarked with many bowl-shaped and water-filled depressions called Carolina bays. Some people think they were made by a long-ago major meteor shower, while others believe they were scraped out by glaciers and filled by glacial melt runoff. However the bays were created, they contain diverse wetland ecosystems that were not easy to cross.

Before 1900, there were no bridges to Long Bay, so ferries were the way to forge wetlands. The major ferry that people paid to use and get across to present-day Myrtle Beach from eastern areas like Florence and Marion was Peachtree Ferry at Socastee. Other Waccamaw River ferries, according to the late historian C.B. Berry, "included Wortham's near Brooksville, just below the North Carolina state line; Star Bluff near Wampee; Conway Ferry across Kingston Lake…Bellamy Landing near the S.C. 9 crossing; Bear Bluff and Reaves Ferry near Nixonville; Hardee Ferry at Savannah Bluff; and Cox's Ferry Below Conway."

In his book *Rum Gully Tales from Tuck 'Em Inn*, Pratt Gasque (1909–1993) described crossing Peachtree Ferry:

> *The ferry was operated by a farmer by the name of Rufus Graham who lived on the east side of the river. Usually he was plowing a field on his farm. We would beat a piece of iron on a plowshare hanging from a tree and Rufus would take his mules to the bar, unhitch them and put them in their stalls. Then he would amble down to the ferry, which was a flat boat only large enough for one automobile. After checking the cables and nodding a greeting to us, he pulled the ferry to our side of the Waccamaw. There he secured the flat to a tree with a stout cable which kept the automobile from pushing the flat away from the bank when it was driven aboard…After paying the toll of fifty cents, we traveled a dirt and corduroy road to Socastee, where we made a stop at Cooper's store to rest after the river crossing, to buy vegetables and check the tires and radiator.*

Cooper's Store still exists beside the Socastee swing bridge, and it is used as a reception hall. It's on the National Register of Historic Places.

Another account of crossing Peachtree Ferry came from the writings of Lucile Burroughs Godfrey (1891–1974), who traveled to the beach with her family from the western part of Horry County. "The long drive on sandy roads required that men and horses rest overnight. Peach Tree Landing, our first stop, is opposite Socastee, which is about five miles from the river. If you had strong lungs, the ferryman answered your call. Otherwise, you banged on an old saw or a piece of metal fastened to a post or tree. The ferry was soon across, and the exciting trip to the far-away beach began."

Kelly Paul Joyner (1915–1999) also recalled fording Peachtree Ferry. "In order to get to Myrtle Beach," she wrote in a 1990 history column, "we had to go to Bucksville and on to Peachtree Ferry. Uncle Luke Duncan…he wasn't really our uncle, but everyone called him 'uncle'…was in charge of

It may have been difficult to get to the beach in the early twentieth century, but the ocean's lure was irresistible. *Horry County Museum, Conway, South Carolina.*

the ferry. As we arrived at the river my father would call out in a loud voice for him to bring the ferry boat over. My father would then drive our car onto the flat boat, and we would be pulled across the river on a steel cable by large oars."

Today, the ferries are gone, and so little remains of any remnants that only people who know what to look for would see them.

SWASHES

Once people got across rivers and swamps and made it to the beach, if they wanted to continue their journey north or south, they had to deal with swashes. Swashes are creeks that end at the coast, and they are natural floodplains. They're like drainage basins that naturally filter storm water impurities. Myrtle Beach has several swashes.

An Englishman and early Methodist preacher, Joseph Pilmoor, wrote in his journal about a five-day journey through Long Bay from February 19 to 25, 1773, which is quoted in a history column by C.B. Berry. Pilmoor describes a harrowing experience forging Singleton Swash:

I took leave of my hospitable friend and went on toward Long Bay…As the tide just suited, I pushed along in hopes of reaching the ford at the eastern end of it before the flowing of the tide, but was too late. There was no house on the beach; to return 15 miles over the bay was very discouraging; to stay all night upon the shore, without anyone to speak to, very disagreeable and to ford the water very dangerous. However, I ventured in but had not gone far before I was at a full stop. The spring-tide came in very rapidly, the waves rolled against the sides of the horse and presently flowed over his back. In this situation, I did not know what I must do…In my distress I lifted up my heart unto God and cried to him for deliverance and immediately it was impressed upon my mind as distinctly as if I had heard a voice saying to me, "Jump down into the water—go along by the side of the horse—take hold of the reins—wade through the water and pull the horse after you." I plunged into the sea immediately and soon found the horse had got into quicksand; the water did not reach up to my breast…I drew him along and escaped safe to the shore. This was one of the most remarkable deliverances of my life. After I had traveled about a mile through the wood, I found a little cottage belonging to a French refugee where I was glad to take up my abode for the night.

In those days, a twenty-mile span on the beach was a "bypass" of Old Kings Highway because traveling on hard-packed beach sand was easier to traverse than the highway's soft sand. The bypass ran from Murrells Inlet in the south to Singleton Swash at the north, and from those points, travelers picked up Old Kings Highway again or headed west.

The Old Kings Highway, a former Native American trail that became a major colonial American north–south route "was the last part of the road between Boston and Savannah to be served by stagecoach," according to the South Carolina State Trails Program. Small spans of the original Old Kings Highway are preserved at two places: Vereen Memorial Gardens in Little River and Meher Baba Spiritual Center at the north end of Myrtle Beach.

Singleton Swash is in the Restaurant Row area of Myrtle Beach, near the present-day Dunes Golf and Beach Club at 9000 North Ocean Boulevard. Singleton Swash has changed names over the years. Maps from the eighteenth and nineteenth centuries show it as Lewis Swash, named for "William Henry Lewis, who died before 1807, [and] was one of the earliest settlers there," according to C.B. Berry. Jeremiah Vareen, who hosted George Washington at his home in 1791, lived near Singleton Swash. In the mid-1800s, Peter Vaught Sr. had a 4,100-acre plantation there, and by 1890, it contained a post office for the surrounding community, known as "Vaught."

During the Civil War, a large salt works was located at Singleton Swash. According to a December 1999 history column in the *Sun News*, "Yankee mariners who destroyed it said it had a 100,000-gallon water tank and pumps powered by horses. About 3,000 bushels of salt were on hand, and it was mixed with sand to make it unusable."

In 1994, C.B. Berry told the story of William Boyd and his wife, who had a salt-making operation before the Civil War. They lived near the massive live oak tree that still grows beside a restaurant in the Galleria shopping center. The couple had a simple setup in which they evaporated seawater to make salt, and Mrs. Boyd "loved that old tree so much that she requested to be buried there."

Many travelers in addition to Joseph Pilmoor have mentioned crossing Singleton Swash on horseback and in carriages and automobiles. President George Washington crossed it in 1791 during his tour of the South, naturalist William Bartram traversed the swash almost two decades earlier and author James Henry Rice had the convertible he was riding in stall there in 1925.

"They were able to save the automobile with the help of a crew of local fishermen," C.B. Berry wrote in August 1993. "Rice, in his book *The Aftermath of Glory*, describes the event."

In the late 1800s and until the 1970s, when development exploded near Singleton Swash, it was common for families from Conway and other outlying areas of Horry County to travel the Long Bay Road that ran from the Star Bluff/Wampee area to Singleton Swash. Often those trips happened after Labor Day, when locals headed to the beach for seine fishing when certain tasty fish were running. "Seines were known to pull in more than 20,000 pounds of mullet and spot, sometimes in a single haul," a November 19, 1999 *Sun News* history note says.

As long as people have populated the South Carolina coast, they have fished the rivers and ocean. Mike Vereen grew up on a farm near Conway, and he remembers going with his father to get fresh fish from beach camps set up for the purpose of seasonal fishing. He recalls fish camps set up at East Cherry Grove and Ocean Drive in North Myrtle Beach and at Singleton Swash, Hurl Rocks, Withers Swash and the south end of present-day Ocean Boulevard.

In the fall, fish made southward runs, and locals knew how to interpret the weather and temperature to anticipate large fish schools. Seine nets with

Sunbathers pitched in to help fishermen pull in large seine nets. *Horry County Museum, Conway, South Carolina.*

ropes and poles on both ends were used, and two or three people got on each end to pull in large fish hauls. Lead weights kept the seines' bottoms weighted, and corks kept the nets' tops floating.

"People would come help them pull the nets in, and they would sell the fish right off the beach," Kathleen Futrell said. "It didn't matter how many pounds you wanted, and they cost ten, fifteen cent a pound. They had a fish fry, fried the fish right up on the beach."

"There were fishing huts all up and down the beach," Vereen said. "They were just poles in the ground and a roof over the top, which would be like maybe a tin roof...They would catch and pile the mullets in one pile and the spots in another pile and the croakers in another pile...they had a weight scale inside that if you wanted five pounds of mullet, whatever it was that you wanted, they'd weigh them."

Vereen, who grew up on a Horry County farm, remembers Singleton Swash as the site of an annual party.

"My grandparents lived right there at Chestnut Hill," he said, "which is part of Singleton Swash. And every year...at the end of the tobacco season, Dad would take all our hands: the croppers, the handers, the stringers, everyone. All the people that helped us gather tobacco...about twelve people, plus our family, and go to Singleton Swash and fish, or probe for flounders, pull a hand seine...and whatever we caught, that's what the people who worked on the farm with us, the ladies and the men, they would prepare and cook it, and we would sit down and eat it. And take a long bench and all of us sit around the benches…and all the children would play ball of some kind…This was like your reward for a good year."

Vereen also remembers going to his grandparents' house on Sunday afternoons and riding in a Jeep to Singleton Swash. He said the area was full of lakes and "the big trees were just bowed over and [there was] nothing but sand dunes for miles and miles and miles."

Midway Swash is around the Springmaid Beach area of Myrtle Beach, at the south end of Ocean Boulevard. Withers Swash (formerly Eight Mile Swash) is at Third Avenue South, Deep Head Swash is near Fifty-second Avenue North, Cane Patch Swash is around Seventy-first Avenue North and Bear Branch Swash is a little north of Eighty-second Avenue North.

C.B. Berry related in a 1992 history column the story of a group of people who made a settlement at Cane Patch Swash about 1835. The story was told to Berry in 1959 by Thomas Walter Livingston (1875–1967), who was told the tale by his aunt, Spicey Ann Reaves Edge (1820–1898).

"She said a caravan of covered wagons stopped at their home (in Dogwood Neck, just across the river from Red Bluff) and requested permission to camp there for a day or two," Berry wrote. "Permission was granted. They were a merry bunch that played the fiddle and danced away the evenings. They were on their way to the coast to establish a settlement. A few years later, they returned and said they were abandoning the settlement, that the water was poisonous and several members of their clan had died."

Livingston speculated to Berry that the group likely drank contaminated surface water at the swash and died from typhoid fever. When he was a young man, Livingston rode by horseback to Cane Patch Swash and "saw remnants of the old stick-and-dirt chimneys in the vicinity."

Before World War II, palatable and safe drinking water often came from artesian wells. However, residents "removed so much water from the Black Creek aquifer that artesian wells are no longer possible," a *Sun News* history note says.

About six hundred German prisoners of war were held from 1943 to 1946 near Cane Patch Swash, which formed a series of "small lakes" between Seventy-first and Seventy-ninth Avenues North.

Deep Head Swash, Floyd wrote, "forms a beautiful tidal lake near the beach before crossing the highway to Pine Lakes. West of the road, behind Rainbow Harbor, is a long narrow lake enjoyed by many homeowners. They will tell you their lake is not a drainage ditch. It is home to numerous ducks, birds and wildlife, a natural sanctuary close to the busy traffic of Kings Highway."

Withers Swash was named for the eighteenth-century family whose members "each had grants in 1765 totaling nearly 3,000 acres in Myrtle Beach," according to C.B. Berry. The Withers had an indigo plantation, raised cattle and produced tar from pine trees, and their home was on a high spot overlooking the swash. The first post office in Myrtle Beach was located near the swash, and it was called the Withers Post Office. Several members of the Withers family are buried in a cemetery at Withers Swash Drive and Collins Street.

C.B. Berry wrote in 1996 that another family prominent in the Withers Swash area was the Todds. A man named Thomas Jefferson Brown, during a 1961 interview, said:

> In 1907, he and his twin brother were plowing the in "Plum Orchard Field" at the south end of what is now Oak Street about 150 feet north of Withers Swash. Frank was digging his plow very deep when it struck and turned some ancient bricks to the surface. Upon further investigation, they found an old brick cellar and surmised that this was probably the site of the Withers house. William T. "Bill" Todd owned that field and his brother, Erasmus Todd, owned the field on the other side of the swash.

The swashes have historically been areas where children have enjoyed playing in their shallow waters that empty into the ocean.

In the 1950s, when Johnny Butler was a young boy growing up in a home on Fifth Avenue South, he played in Withers Swash, which empties at a stretch of beach formerly referred to as Spivey Beach (named for the Spivey family of Conway). "In the mid to late 1920s," the Myrtle Beach Comprehensive Plan says, "Senator D.A. Spivey of the Horry Land Improvement Company began buying land in this area, which extended approximately from 1st Avenue South to 17th Avenue South and included the blocks between the ocean and Oak Street. Spivey Beach did not really begin to develop, however, until the 1940s and 1950s."

"It was undeveloped, like a big swim hole," Butler said. "My house is still by the little pond…It's actually a drain pond for the south end of Myrtle Beach. When I had my grocery store there, I could walk right back out to the canal and catch flounder. We didn't give a thought to the drainage. It was a good wholesome lifestyle."

Ann Vereen grew up in Conway, but her father built a beach house near Withers Swash. She also remembers playing there in the 1940s and '50s.

Withers Swash, shown here in 2014, used to be a wildlife haven where residents fished and swam. *Photo by Becky Billingsley.*

"That's where we played," she said, "because that area was just beautiful before [the land was purchased for] an amusement park…There was a wooden pavilion there, right where the water park is now."

But development and a huge influx of seasonal visitors polluted Withers Swash. A 1973 article in the *Florence Morning News* said:

> *Along Highway 17 North, one remaining section of natural marshland known as Spivey's Swash is now almost completely surrounded by campgrounds, homesites and recreational facilities. Less than five years ago the marsh was a haven for wildlife but area residents point out that in 1973 only an occasional bird can be seen. Myrtle Beach Airport's aviation traffic crosses the marshland just seconds after take-off.*

In 1991, Blanche Floyd wrote, "Today, Withers Swash lies contaminated and trash-laden, its waters dark and murky with debris. The S.C. Department of Health and Environmental Control has classified the swash as 'grossly polluted' by stormwater drainage, development along its banks, and neglected litter. It has the poorest water quality of any marsh along the Grand Strand, destroying its fragile ecology."

The days of allowing children to play in swash waters have been lost because the waters are too polluted. In 2012, a project was implemented by personnel at Coastal Carolina University to track sources of fecal pollution at fourteen sites around the Withers Swash sub-watershed. The site was chosen because it is "highly contaminated with [fecal indicator bacteria]."

While today much of Withers Swash is lost to development and pollution, especially where it ends at the beach, eleven acres of its wetlands are preserved inland at Withers Swash Park. It has a fishing pier, picnic shelter, playground and walking trails. A Withers Swash boardwalk goes through Family Kingdom Amusement Park, and a Withers Swash neighborhood west of Kings Highway has several vintage homes.

The city of Myrtle Beach has a twenty-five-year plan that will incorporate the Withers Swash corridor to include an "integrated green infrastructure" where "introduction of a bioswale median cleans stormwater, street trees reduce heat island effect and provides shaded outdoor spaces, rain gardens create bladder conditions retaining initial stormwater and improving water quality."

"Withers Swash…drains one-third of the city," Myrtle Beach Planning director Jack Walker said. "When you get beyond Kings Highway there are tributaries for miles that drain in that direction. That's a natural and cultural resource."

HURL (HEARL) ROCKS

Hearl Rocks was a distinctive black coquina rock formation near Twentieth Avenue South in Myrtle Beach. They were "the only naturally occurring rocks on the South Carolina coast," wrote author Rick Simmons. Historian Blanche Floyd wrote in 1991 that the rocks were named for a local landowner with the surname of Hearl who settled in the Socastee area before the American Revolution. In July 1765, naturalist John Bartram saw Hearl Rocks and described them as "a solid sheet of concrete—so soft as with a sharp knife to cut a little hole in it." In the 1770s, his son, William Bartram, noted the "cliffs of rocks."

Sometime in the early twentieth century, a new landowner, Margaret Anne Klein, changed the spelling to Hurl Rocks because of the way waves hurled onto them. Hurl Rocks had eroded by then, but Floyd wrote that "in the early 1900s, the rocks stood three to six feet tall, a high point along the flat sandy beach."

In 1941, Hurl Rocks was the site of an art colony at Hurlcote, the former home of Margaret Anne Klein. "Writers and painters from South Carolina, Georgia, Virginia, New York and Massachusetts have visited here and found inspiration," an article in the September 3, 1941 edition of the *Aiken Standard and Review* says. "An art colony is a fitting memorial to Miss Klein, dramatic reader and journalist who always cultivated the beautiful and best in mankind." Artist and poetess Talulah Lemmon, a Conway native, also had a home at Hurl Rocks called Cherokee Place. She and her husband, Ensign Henry Clemson MacInvaill Jr., went on in 1947 to help open the Pink House Restaurant, formerly at 4301 North Kings Highway in Myrtle Beach.

Through the ages, Hurl Rocks was a favorite place for families to picnic during the day and for young couples to "watch submarine races" at night.

The rocks were further eroded by time and weather and covered by beach nourishment. Hurl Rocks was still barely visible at low tide in the late 1990s, but today, it is lost; what's left of it is covered by sand. A pocket park on Ocean Boulevard commemorates Hurl Rocks; it was the city's first oceanfront park and was acquired in the 1970s.

DENSE VEGETATION

Early visitors passed through and traveled beside growths of swamp magnolias, yaupon, wax myrtles, cedars, loblolly and longleaf pines, oak trees and more, and they grew right down to where giant sand dunes provided a beach buffer. Part of Long Bay was called Yaupon Beach, near the present-day Yaupon Drive that extends from Withers Swash to Twenty-ninth Avenue South. Blanche Floyd wrote in 1993 that the area was named for its "thick growth of native yaupon bushes and trees, with their bright red winter berries. American Indians reportedly used the poisonous berries in coming of age ceremonies for their young men, to prove their manhood."

Carolina bays throughout Horry County are bowl-shaped wetlands that contain unique ecosystems found nowhere else. C.B. Berry wrote in 1995 that the bays used to be called pocosins.

"A sandy rim that ranges six to eight feet above the floor usually surrounds these bays," Berry wrote, "which are oriented from northwest to southeast and the vegetation growing inside include sweet bay, red bay, loblolly bay, blueberries, holly and the bamboo greenbrier vine. This briar is a bane to the woodsman as well as many homeowners and is often referred to as 'Confederate barbed wire.' Also growing there are the famous carnivorous pitcher plant and Venus fly trap."

Many bays still exist, but many others were filled in for development and are lost.

The remaining bays are losing their unique plants such as Venus' flytraps. The North Carolina History Project states, "Only a few hundred carnivorous plants are on Earth and only six of those are native to the United States. One is the Venus Flytrap." In 2013, each flytrap was worth twenty dollars, making their theft irresistible for some poachers. An hour north of Myrtle Beach at Alderman Park in Wilmington, North Carolina, someone stole 90 percent of the park's state-protected Venus' flytraps—about 1,500 plants—in May 2013.

The wax myrtles for which Myrtle Beach is named are also disappearing as residential and commercial construction replaces them with grass lawns and nonnative trees, shrubs and flowers. However, there are many homes within the city limits, especially between Ocean Boulevard and Kings Highway, that have delightful, thick native foliage composed of the trees, shrubs, grasses and flowers that used to blanket the formerly isolated area.

"One of my earliest memories actually of Myrtle Beach," Myrtle Beach local Billy Wright said, "is my grandmother lived on Thirty-seventh Avenue, and I remember…turning in on Thirty-seventh off the highway and…you could see the ocean of course, and the trees cover up the avenue…so it was like you're looking down a cave and all of a sudden there's the ocean."

That famous sight can still be appreciated on Thirty-seventh Avenue North and surrounding numbered streets where vintage beach cottages line streets with no hotels blocking their beach views.

2
HURRICANES

There's a good reason the South Carolina coastline is concave: eons of hurricanes have slammed into it. During colonial times, hurricanes were called September gales "probably because the ones people remembered and wrote about were those which damaged or destroyed crops just before they were to be harvested," according to the South Carolina State Climatology Office.

Official records of South Carolina hurricanes have been kept since 1871, and they had names starting in 1950. Unofficial records were kept prior to 1871, and Hobcaw Barony senior historian Lee Brockington wrote in 1990 about "gales of wind" that affected Spanish privateers in the 1740s.

A storm recorded in 1752 in Georgetown County was "called a 'heavy blow'," Blanche Floyd wrote in 1995. "This storm greatly damaged the small, weak settlements of Georgetown and Kingston on the Waccamaw (Conway). Wind and water surge ruined dams and dikes of rice plantations on Waccamaw Neck and Pee Dee River Lands."

In 1822, a storm washed away the home of the Withers family near present-day Third Avenue South in Myrtle Beach. Blanche Floyd shared that hurricane story in a column she wrote in 1991:

> In 1822, a hurricane came ashore after three days of heavy rains, and the storm surge coincided with the high tide. The water rushed in as far as the Withers house. Eighteen people had taken refuge inside. According to "The Independent Republic: A Survey History of Horry County, S.C.," a sudden surge of water lifted the house off its foundation and floated it

into the swash and out to sea. The windows shone brightly with the light of candles and lamps, making it look like a ship sailing away. Reportedly, the house broke up, and all 18 people lost their lives…The house was gone, and the fields grew up in pine and scrub oak trees.

Lee Brockington said the 1822 storm "claimed 300 lives, including entire families. The area was caught in the dangerous northeast semicircle of the storm, much as McClellanville was with Hugo."

In those early days, hurricanes were all the more terrifying because no one knew with certainty they were coming or how strong the storms would be. In the 1800s, hurricanes could hit so suddenly, Brockington wrote, that "area rice planters erected brick storm towers in the rice fields for people to climb to escape rising waters."

Buried deep in the sands of Myrtle Beach at about Forty-third Avenue North are the remains of one of about seventy ships that were lost during the great storm of August 1893. The *Freeda A. Wyley* was, according to Blanche Floyd in a 1991 column, "a 507-ton barkentine—a three-masted vessel—with a square rigged foremast and two fore-and-aft rigged sails."

The ship was hauling lumber from Mississippi to New York when it sailed into the storm. Late on the evening of August 28, 1893, the ship "was reported burning fiercely off Frying Pan Shoals, near the mouth of the Cape Fear River. No one knows what started the blaze, but in such a violent storm, an upset galley stove or lantern could have ignited the fire." The tattered and water-swollen captain's log was found, and the last entry, dated August 29, said, "Heaven help us." After the *Freeda A. Wyley* burned to the water line, its hull drifted until it came to rest at Myrtle Beach. Beach nourishment has covered the wood skeleton, and it's no longer visible.

A hurricane on October 13, 1893, caused a "memorable tidal wave" that erased all houses but one at Magnolia Beach, which is present-day Litchfield Beach to the south of Myrtle Beach. Several hundred people are believed to have died along the South Carolina coast.

The National Oceanic and Atmospheric Administration (NOAA) has a Historical Hurricane Tracker on its website, and if you put Myrtle Beach into the location field, you'll see a confetti rainbow of storm tracks crisscross the city. Most were tropical storms, but there are enough Category 1–4 hurricane tracks to give pause.

Two Category 4 hurricanes that severely impacted Myrtle Beach include Hazel in October 1954 and Hugo in September 1989. Hazel had 106-mile-per-hour winds and a 16.9-foot storm surge, according to the

Ann Vereen said the aftermath of Hurricane Hazel "was like an atomic bomb had gone off." *Horry County Museum, Conway, South Carolina.*

South Carolina Department of Natural Resources. A December 1955 report from NOAA says, "Wind estimates from several points between Myrtle Beach and Cape Fear varied from 130 to 150 m.p.h. The devastation along the North and South Carolina beaches was staggering. Every pier in a distance of 170 miles of coastline was demolished and whole lines of beach homes literally disappeared. In some places the tide was over 17 feet higher than mean low water." The Myrtle Beach Comprehensive Plan says, "Many of the small cottages and boarding houses that had typified Myrtle Beach's early oceanfront development north to the Myrtle Heights section were destroyed by the storm and replaced by small, 20–40 room motel operations."

Ann Vereen was eleven years old when Hurricane Hazel struck the Myrtle Beach area.

"It was so scary, so devastating," she said in November 2013 at her oceanfront home at the south end of Myrtle Beach.

We went to my grandmother's house on Fourth Avenue in Conway. She baked a ham and a pound cake—she always cooked before a storm. Trees were down everywhere. Live oaks, big trees. Then we found out what had

Hurricane Hazel upended lives for a while, and then Myrtle Beach had a construction boom. *Peggy Mishoe collection.*

actually happened at the beach. All the electric lines were down, and debris was everywhere. The houses along the beach were down; it was like an atomic bomb had gone off. We hadn't had such a strong storm for more than fifty years.

Residents had little warning of Hazel's severity. Johnny Butler was in elementary school at the time, and his father was a Myrtle Beach City police officer. His father woke him up late that night and told him to shelter with his mother at Myrtle Beach Grade School, which was located at Fifth Avenue South where the post office is now.

Blanche Floyd wrote that North Myrtle Beach "Police Chief Merlin Bellamy was a hero in Hurricane Hazel when the storm turned unexpectedly at sea in the early morning hours. He and six other men went from door to door, rushing Ocean Drive people out of the danger zone. The 'eye' of the hurricane came ashore at Ocean Drive, flattening every waterfront structure down the coast, but 2,000 people had found places of safety."

Kelly Paul Joyner was a mother of five sons, two of whom were in college, when late on October 14, 1954, they had a phone call, she wrote in 1992.

Her husband, Joe Joyner, was the city's director of public works, and he was instructed to go to city hall and set up a shelter:

> *The police were sent up and down Ocean Boulevard and all over town with a bullhorn waking people and warning everyone to seek shelter at The Ocean Forest Hotel, Myrtle Beach Elementary School and First Presbyterian Church. At the height of the storm, the tide was at its highest. Joe let [two of our sons] ride with him until he had to bring them home. I didn't leave our home. I felt I couldn't rest on the pews at the church with a 2-year-old child and another on the way. After the storm, I took my children down to the end of 18th Avenue North. Refrigerators, couches and everything imaginable was washed up on the boulevard. You couldn't even drive on it. Looters converged on the beach immediately until the National Guard was called in. The national news reported that "Myrtle Beach, South Carolina, was blown away." Well, some of that was true. Beach houses were literally blown away, but some said that Hazel was the best thing that happened to Myrtle Beach because hotels and homes were rebuilt bigger and better.*

Wynness Thomas of Conway told her Hurricane Hazel story in a 1993 *Sun News* history column:

> *On the morning of Oct. 15, 1954, we were awakened by our neighbor about daybreak, telling us that Hurricane Hazel was expected to hit Myrtle Beach. We decided to drive to the home of Fred's parents in the Nixonville community….Nixonville is only about six miles directly from the coast, but because of the waterway, cars must travel by U.S. 501 and S.C. 90…We arrived safely at the Thomas home before the storm hit. As the wind began to increase, the large frame house creaked and groaned but stayed intact. Fred and his father spent much time on the spacious front porch watching the fury of the hurricane and noting the direction of the wind as it shifted. I remember looking at the neighbor's house with a sharp-pointed roof during the heavy deluge. The wind was blowing at such an angle that the water scooped upward from the bottom to the top of the roof, producing a water fountain effect. During the afternoon the hurricane moved on and we drove anxiously home, not knowing what to expect. We arrived at our little cottage with the sun shining bright, to find a few pinecones in the front yard, and everything undamaged. Many people were not so fortunate. With the power off, everything was at a standstill.*

Marcus Smith also remembered an early morning wake-up call at his home on Thirty-eighth Avenue North. "At 4 a.m. on the morning of Oct. 15, the continuous ringing of our doorbell awakened us from a deep sleep. When I opened the door…our friend informed us the hurricane had stalled and turned toward the coast. He advised us to leave immediately."

Smith and his wife were expecting their first child in a few weeks, and they understood that the low pressure in hurricanes could induce premature labor. They drove to Smith's parents' house in Conway, which was a few blocks from the hospital. "As we traveled down Kings Highway, city and county patrol officers passed us, with sirens screaming, alerting people of impending danger." The weather was already bad. Smith described "water-filled gorges on both sides of the road" and said that "gale force winds rocked the car and sheets of heavy rain blasted the windshield."

The young couple made it to Conway at 5:00 a.m. and listened to the radio. Myrtle Beach's WMYB had already lost its power at midnight. By 6:30 a.m., the wind had increased, water had crossed Ocean Boulevard and fishing piers were destroyed. People were advised that Hurricane Hazel would hit the coast at 10:00 a.m., at high tide, with winds of 130 miles per hour.

By noon, it was over. The Smiths returned to the beach and went to the police department, where they had to get a resident's pass to go to their home. "On the oceanfront, many homes, cottages and guest houses were undermined," Smith wrote. "Dunes were leveled, with massive beach erosion. The oceanfront wooden boardwalk, which extended from 27th Avenue North to Third Avenue South, floated out to sea. Slabs of concrete, once the sidewalk that ran the length of The Pavilion and amusement section, were lifted like sheets of paper and hurled into beachside stores."

"Hazel destroyed 273 houses in Myrtle Beach," Helen Milliken wrote in *From the Beginning: A History of the Burroughs & Chapin Company*, "and 80 percent of waterfront development. Property damage along the Grand Strand was estimated at $24 million."

Nine fishing piers up and down the Grand Strand were gone. Sand dunes were flattened. Building debris from first-row destruction was scattered everywhere, including on the roads. Statewide, damage estimates were $27 million.

Cleanup began quickly, and by the tourist season of 1955, Myrtle Beach was beyond repaired—it was growing.

Barbara Stokes wrote in *Greetings from…Myrtle Beach: A History, 1900–1980*:

> *Construction in 1955 was not limited to properties affected by Hurricane Hazel. More than $2 million was spent in the coming year on new construction, which included 485 new rooms in motor court and hotel additions, apartments and apartment hotels, as well as the modernization and expansion of guest houses and motor courts. Most of this construction would have been done even if Hurricane Hazel had not blown through Horry County. However, the types of buildings that replaced those destroyed on the beach emphasized to people the differences in Myrtle Beach before and after Hurricane Hazel—the transition from a quaint summer colony to a high-rise resort city.*

The 2009 Horry County Historic Resources Survey notes that Hazel blew away many wood-framed "apartment buildings, travel courts and beach homes" and replacement construction was "sturdy, concrete block and brick motels."

Since 1901, eight hurricanes impacting the South Carolina coast were Category 2 or higher, but none transformed Myrtle Beach more than Hazel. It was a game-changer. A population surge happened after World War II with many new people moving to town to open businesses to serve the speedily growing tourist population. From 1940 to 1950, Myrtle Beach's population doubled to 3,345 residents. A newspaper mention of Myrtle Beach with regards to the upcoming Fourth of July holiday says South Carolina's beaches were "led by Myrtle Beach, whose spectacular development during the past two decades has been something phenomenal, the growth of beaches along the Horry coast has provided beach resorts which compare favorably with any offered along the entire length of the Eastern Seaboard." It was inevitable that Myrtle Beach would change and grow, but the thoroughness with which Hazel wiped the slate clean on the oceanfront sped up the process of turning Myrtle Beach from a slow-paced seaside resort to an area of fast-paced and almost unchecked growth.

Hurricanes are always a variable in building anything in Myrtle Beach. A severe reminder came in 1989 with Hurricane Hugo. The worst destruction from Hugo was a little south of Myrtle Beach, but the Category 4 storm impacted the city harshly. Michelle Johnson Householder was glad her family didn't ride it out close to the coast:

> *I had just graduated from Myrtle Beach High. We stayed home. My aunt, who lives just across the waterway in Carolina Lakes, was going to stay*

[with us], *but at the very last minute, we went to her house. I remember opening the front door in the middle of the night—because it all happened at night—and I could hear trees snapping. The next morning, all the trees were topped. Every tree, everywhere was just topped off. It was weird. Early the next morning, when it* [had] *died down a little bit, we got back across the border* [and our yard] *was trashed. We didn't lose one shingle, though. We lived by the Back Gate off Emory Road. It took seven people two eight-hour days to clean up our yard. I remember going to Surfside, and it was so heart wrenching seeing the houses in the middle of the street where they had been washed off the stilts. I remember we just couldn't believe what we were seeing…there was a toilet sitting there in the middle of the street. It was so sad. I remember seeing a baby crib out there. All their stuff was just everywhere. They had the National Guard* [come]; *they finally got there and blocked people from going down those streets to prevent looters. It was horrible. It makes me want to cry whenever I think about it now.*

3

TRAINS, BRIDGES AND AUTOMOBILES

Once it became easier to get to Myrtle Beach, much of the forested landscape was dramatically altered.

The railroad came to Conway in late 1887, from Wilmington, North Carolina, along with the Western Union telegraph, but it was another thirteen years before trains brought visitors to Myrtle Beach.

"Ox cart and wagon were the primary means of ground travel," according to the written history of the Burroughs & Chapin Company (formerly the Myrtle Beach Farms Company and Burroughs & Collins Company, which merged to form Burroughs & Chapin Company, Inc., in 1990), "and with poor-quality roads, the going was rough. Some stagecoaches traveled through the county, delivering mail or passengers. Affluent families drove buggies."

Railroads were the first avenues that increased population in Myrtle Beach. "In 1896…F.G. Burroughs and his son, Franklin Augustus, surveyed a straight line from Conway some 14 miles to the beach in preparation for a planned railroad." Construction began in 1899, and at that time, Myrtle Beach was called New Town, as opposed to the "old town," which was Conway. Service on the Conway and Seashore Railroad from Conway to New Town began on May 1, 1900, "with two wood-burning locomotives, two second-hand passenger cars…and a few freight cars. The engine pulling the ragtag menagerie was affectionately dubbed The Black Maria." The railroad ended at an area called Pine Island, and there's still a Pine Island Road in Myrtle Beach that extends from U.S. 17, by Coastal Grand Mall, toward the beach.

The two train cars held about 150 people and were open sided. Passengers had to watch for embers from the steam engine to avoid pitting their clothing with burn holes.

From 1900 to 1904, a ferry ride across the Waccamaw River was part of the train trip to the beach until Burroughs & Collins built a train bridge. In 1904, the rail company changed its name to the Conway, Coast and Western Railroad, and in 1905, it was sold.

A 1955 article that ran in the *Myrtle Beach Sun News* describes how

> *the railroad…came in close by the pavilion and continued on to the beach where it stopped near a small beach shelter. This railroad was an extension of the present* [in 1955] *railway, which now stops at the Atlantic Coastline Terminal. "The beach shed looked like a country depot and excursion trains from inland brought visitors to the beach,"* [Casper L. Benton] *recalls. "Fish camps were located where the present amusement center lies. There was no law in those days. This arrival of the excursion trains usually resulted in free-for-alls between the natives and the visitors," Mr. Benton said. He tells how the natives met the train and, "picked fights with the newcomers."*

The first automobile arrived in Conway in 1906, and by 1911, Horry County residents owned 19 of the 5,355 cars registered in South Carolina.

Before the Myrtle Beach Pavilion had an amusement park, the train to the beach ended near Eighth Avenue North. *Horry County Museum, Conway, South Carolina.*

Automobiles could be driven on the beach in the 1920s. *Horry County Museum, Conway, South Carolina.*

"Road travel improved when a 1904 drawbridge and a 1912 swing truss bridge were constructed over the Waccamaw River to connect routes from Conway along the railroad and along the dirt road towards Socastee and ultimately the beach," the 2009 Horry County Historic Resources Survey says. "In 1914, the route to Myrtle Beach was completed and residents enjoyed dancing in the Pavilion, a large, shingled, wood frame structure, or walking along the wood boardwalk, which connected small beach cottages."

"The development of Myrtle Beach means the early completion of the Coastal Highway from Wilmington to Charleston," states a June 14, 1929 article in the *Aiken Standard*. "The editor of The *News & Courier* in describing the road from Charleston to Myrtle Beach says: 'in one hundred miles, outside of Georgetown, is scarcely a dwelling visible from the road that cost as much as $3000. Most of the cabins are squalid, unpainted, hopeless of outlook.' This will change overnight, almost, with the development of Myrtle Beach and the hardsurfacing of the road from there to Charleston." Also in 1929, the Myrtle Beach Comprehensive Plan says "the old Conway Highway from Socastee to Myrtle Beach, including Broadway, East Broadway, and 9th Avenue North, was paved with rock and asphalt. Ocean Drive from 9th Avenue North to Ocean Plaza (14th avenue North area) was also paved."

A late 1930s hard-surface road leading from the Conway bridge to Myrtle Beach helped travelers even more. J. Marcus Smith explained in 1995 what that route was like.

In the mid-1930s, summer traffic from the west traveled through Marion, Aynor, Cool Spring and Homewood before arriving in Conway. Beach-bound tourists, along with locals, traveled down Main Street to Third Avenue and made a left turn at the Town Hall. After one block, motorists turned right at Kingston Presbyterian Church and, 100 yards away, a left turn at the Conway Electric and Ice Company building. Long-time Conway residents remember the noisy, wooden-plank bridge across the mouth of Kingston Lake, which was the next step on the road to Myrtle Beach...The bridge no longer exists. [From the other side of the former Kingston Lake Bridge] *we followed the old road a quarter of a mile and observed the curve approaching the Waccamaw River. We located the site where the drawbridge, which was built prior to 1920, once stood. The bridge had crossed at the narrowest part of the river, which had high banks on both sides. As we observed some remaining pilings, we saw the nearby trestle bridge that still stands at the original site of the early train route...The original narrow roadway rambled through swampy land.*

Smith said that old roadway to the beach was often impassable due to high water. It ran by the former O.L. Williams Veneer Manufacturing plant and the Stilley Mill, which produced plywood. As the road approached Red Hill, there was another bridge and a third set of train tracks, and then the road to the beach took the path of today's SC 544. "The old road curved to the left in Socastee and continued for nine miles," Smith wrote, "entering downtown Myrtle Beach by West Broadway."

As getting to Myrtle Beach became easier, the crowds increased. A June 1930 article in the *Florence Morning News* described events for the upcoming Fourth of July week, when "between 15,000 and 20,000 people are expected to enjoy the festivities." They included a tea dance and an "elaborate fireworks display on the beach" followed by "a grand ball."

Another travel boon, in the form of boat travel, came in 1936, when the Intracoastal Waterway was completed. Its dedication was held at the waterway swing bridge at Socastee.

Before the waterway was finished, the old Long Bay Road that ran between northwest Horry County and Myrtle Beach was a popular beach route. However, that road was lost when the waterway cut it off, and it was

If You Must Go—

Schedules

Bus Schedule:

Leave for Charlotte, N. C.: 8:15 a.m., 12:15 p.m., 3:15 p.m., 6:00 p.m.

Leave for Raleigh, N. C.: 2:50 p.m., 6:00 p.m.

Leave for Columbia, S. C.: 9:20 a.m., 2:40 p.m., 6:00 p.m.,

Arrive from Charlotte, N. C.: 10:30 a.m., 1:00 p.m., 5:30 p.m., 10:55 p.m.

On Fridays and Saturdays special Express from Charlotte, arriving in Myrtle Beach at 9:30 p.m.

Arrive from Columbia, S. C.: 2:25 p.m., 9:25 p.m.

Arrive from Raleigh, N. C.: 1:25 p.m.

LOCAL BUS SCHEDULE

Myrtle Beach Transit Co.

Leaving every hour on the hour from the Bus Station next to Chamber of Commerce office. Going to Lakeside Court on N. Kings Hwy. Picking up passengers in the Ocean Forest section and return down Kings Hwy. Leaving every hour on the hour from the Bus Station next to Chamber of Commerce office. Going to the Airport, coming up Kings Hwy. to 30th Ave., where it turns down Ocean Blvd.

In 1955, Myrtle Beach had a convenient bus route. *Author's collection.*

further lost when it and 55,854 surrounding acres were used during World War II as a military bombing and gunnery range. C.B. Berry described it in a 1993 column as being "bounded north by S.C. 90; east by S.C. 9; south by the Intracoastal Waterway and west by the Atlantic Coastline Railway. This became a practice range for aircraft gunners and bombers during the war. All residents and buildings had been removed and all private activities ceased and this giant area was used exclusively for military practice activities."

Berry wrote that some of the bomb craters were still visible in 1993, and "although the War Department returned most of the land to former owners, it has never recovered. The Long Bay Road now terminates near an old cattle dip vat at the northwestern boundary of the Skyway Golf Course" in the Restaurant Row area of Myrtle Beach.

A huge leap in easy driving access to Myrtle Beach came on November 10, 1948, when chief highway commissioner Claude R. McMillan cut the ribbon at the grand opening of U.S. 501, which connected Conway and Myrtle Beach. The road cut the twenty-one-mile driving distance from Conway to the beach, via the old Socastee road, to fourteen miles. Eleven years later, in 1959, the U.S. 501/Church Street bypass diverted much beach traffic from historic downtown Conway.

Many more roads have been constructed and paved since then to handle millions of annual visitors. Locals are grateful when new roads ease traffic snarls, but at the same time, they rue the resulting loss of open land and vegetation sacrificed to make room for them.

4

BEACH RETREATS

In 1881, local business Burroughs & Collins bought 3,654 acres from Dusenbury & Sarvis in the New Town area. Part of that purchase is what is now a shopping/dining/entertainment complex called Broadway at the Beach, which present-day Burroughs & Chapin Co. still owns. The Withers family of the Withers Swash area had previously owned much of the land, and some was purchased from the heirs of plantation owner Joshua Ward.

In 1900, when the train came to New Town, the tiny community received a new name. The Myrtle Beach Comprehensive Plan says, "One evening, a group of people from Conway decided to vote on a name for New Town. Mrs. F.G. Burroughs submitted the name, Myrtle Beach, because of the abundance of native myrtle bushes in the area." The runner-up name was Edgewater.

As the Myrtle Beach area slowly became populated, some structures were as fleeting as the seasons. Crude shacks used tree boughs to shade beach-goers and fishermen from the sun, and they were swept away with the first strong wind.

When more permanent structures were built, they were mostly seasonal beach homes. "The new beach homes were usually one story, of wood construction, with medium pitched gable roofs and low-pitched porch roofs. Crowded among wax myrtle shrubs and other foliage, the somewhat haphazard placement of buildings was very different from the dense and rigidly aligned development of successive years," the 2009 Horry County Historic Resources Survey says. However, it goes on to say, "There are apparently no existing examples of the earliest beach cottages, though some

None of the earliest beach homes still exist. *Horry County Museum, Conway, South Carolina.*

homes, which likely date to the 1930s, carry the low and wide hipped roof that was popular in homes from the late 1910s and 1920s."

Barbara Horner, a Myrtle Beach resident who was the archivist at the *Sun News* daily newspaper for twenty years, said those roofs were commonly called umbrella roofs.

Small communities were absorbed into Myrtle Beach, including one around Withers Swash at Third Avenue South and one called Sandridge that extended between Seventeenth Avenue South and Third Avenue North. Some people who lived in Dogwood Neck and Socastee migrated to Myrtle Beach.

In 1905, Myrtle Beach Farms Company (a partnership between Franklin G. Burroughs's heirs and northern investor Simeon B. Chapin) started selling oceanfront lots for $25 each. If landowners built a home on the lot worth at least $500, a second lot was free. The A.W. Barrett family of Conway built one of the first oceanfront cottages, and the construction bill was $75. These homes and lots were reserved for Caucasian people because "a 'deadline' formed in Horry County, running from the north-central town of Loris to the western town of Aynor, and any African-American who did not already live west of the line was not allowed to cross it," according to the 2009 Horry County historic property survey.

Burroughs & Collins continued to acquire property. The Myrtle Beach Comprehensive Plan says, "According to Edward Burroughs' 1971 column in The *Independent Republic* quarterly, the company had by 1906 accumulated over 100,000 acres of land including ten miles of beach front property, from the location of the former Ocean Forest Hotel to around 1st Avenue South. Burroughs also speculated that, from 1900 until the start of World War I, somewhere between fifteen to twenty beachfront cottages were built."

Several hundred homes were built by 1925, and Myrtle Beach had about 200 permanent residents. A 1926 advertisement in the *Florence Morning News* for the Myrtle Beach Sales real estate company says:

> *The nights are featured by numerous pleasant social gatherings of congenial, substantial people, with whom you will delight to mingle. The days are full of joys and pleasures in the form of surf bathing, rowing, yachting, fishing, riding, driving, dancing, hunting (in season) and shortly golf and tennis will be added. You could hardly please your family more than by selecting a lot and building a home at Myrtle Beach. Already it is a thriving resort city, with hotel and annexes, pavilion, bath house, club, 2 mile board walk, new streets and highways, cement sidewalks and a white way, water and electricity available. Beautiful home sites are being sold in the hotel section every day except Sunday. Prices $400 and up; liberal terms.*

The vice-president and executive manager of Myrtle Beach Sales Co. was Brigadier General H.B. Springs, and the property he sold was referred to as Myrtle Beach Estates.

A well-known writer of the day, J. Allen Dunn, visited Myrtle Beach in 1927 and was paraphrased by the *Aiken Standard* as saying, "He had never seen anything like it so far as the climate, elevation, placidity of the ocean and accessibility of the approach to the beach are concerned. In fact, Mr. Dunn and his party are so charmed with the place that they expect to remain here several days longer than originally planned. Reports in New York City about Myrtle Beach caused them to come here. They declare it is superior to the Riviera in Italy."

By 1938, Myrtle Beach had enough people living there to need a police force and other civic services. The town was incorporated, and Myrtle Beach had its first mayor, Dr. W.L. Harrelson.

About this time, larger two-story homes were being built, and the 2009 architectural survey says they were "most often of wood construction with clapboard siding and low pitched hip or gable roofs, with exposed rafters in the eaves...Several homes directly faced the ocean, and development occurred in a northwesterly direction behind the first line of ocean front residences." Some homes built in Myrtle Beach from the 1920s through the 1950s were the Bungalow and Minimal Traditionalist styles, but *the more cosmopolitan neighborhoods growing up in Myrtle Beach displayed the circa 1950 Colonial Revival style, often with an impression porch replete with colossal columns, symmetrical fenestration, and an elaborate door surround. With extremely shallow eaves, multi-paned sash windows, and often two stories, these wood frame homes created neighborhoods of wealthy residents with relatively high styled homes.*

Often these homes had small square buildings behind them, or behind their garages, to house domestic servants.

Starting in 1940, Barbara Horner's family owned property in the area of Seventy-sixth Avenue North. In those days the numbered streets stopped there, and that part of town was considered to be living in the country. Her father paid about $800 apiece for the lots. As her parents aged, they spent winters at their Myrtle Beach home, and her mother "brought all of her servants with her. The back end of this house was a big carport, and she had her maid's quarters [behind it]."

"By the mid-1950s," the 2009 historic survey says, "the coastal beaches of the entire stretch along Horry County were called the 'Grand Strand,' a nickname created by local businessman Claude Dunnagan." The pace of growth slowed during the 1960s, and "the majority of Horry developed along existing roads as newer homes simply filled in large gaps left by the agrarian heritage of vast acreage between homes…This type of growth created an unusual streetscape, fitting in newer brick ranch style homes, sprawling across their lots, with smaller Bungalow cottages or older tenant houses, generally wood framed with clapboard siding."

Ranch-style homes were constructed in the 1950s through the 1980s, and several inland neighborhoods full of them were built to house personnel working at the Myrtle Beach U.S. Air Force Base. After Hazel caused widespread oceanfront destruction in 1954, beach homes raised on stilts became prevalent.

Some historic homes still exist in Myrtle Beach as of spring 2014, and while dozens of houses, including whole districts of homes, are recommended by the Horry County Board of Architectural Review to be on the National Register of Historic Places, only a handful are. A notable group of fifteen homes on the NRHP is on Ocean Boulevard between Thirty-second and Forty-sixth Avenues North in what's called the Myrtle Heights–Oak Park Historic District. The 2009 historic property survey says this small number of houses on the register is of concern:

Within Horry County there are many fine historic homes, primarily concentrated within urban areas like Conway, Loris, or the coast. While Conway boasts a fine collection of homes and an obvious respect for their preservation, towns such as Loris and Myrtle Beach have no current preservation ordinances in place to protect their historic structures. This is of special concern along the coast, as ever-expanding development has already erased block after block of historic beach cottages dating from the early 1900s, replacing them with modern structures. The few examples of homes that still exist along Ocean Boulevard, the main north to south street following the beach line from Surfside Beach to Cherry Grove Beach in the north, stand out strangely among their new commercial and hotel neighbors. Only two homes on Ocean Boulevard retain the long, sloping roofline popular in 1920s beach cottages, the Victory motel office at 202 South Ocean Boulevard (Site 2889) and its neighbor, 106 South Ocean Boulevard (Site 2890). Both are crowded by modern development, their second-row views of the ocean blocked by high-rise hotels. Part of the reason visitors believe Myrtle Beach "doesn't have any historic sites" is because large swaths of its structures have been removed, demolishing historic buildings that created continuity in the streetscape. Now, single historic homes appear severely out of place among modern high rises, hotels and condominiums. Owners of the homes receive constant requests to sell their precious real estate, while at the same time dealing with the rising tax and insurance costs associated with their ever-changing neighborhood. Current zoning, which allows for multiple stories, makes the few remaining homes targets for demolition, as their lots could be developed with the full potential that the current zoning allows.

Barbara Horner understands some developers' persistence in obtaining oceanfront land. For many years, her father owned the entire block of Seventy-sixth Avenue North from Kings Highway to the beach. When he passed away, Horner inherited the family's personal beach house, built in 1945, on a street full of historically significant early beach homes. Her neighbors included North Carolina's lieutenant governor and state treasurer. In the mid-1970s, Horner and fellow residents learned of news that foretold their neighborhood's destruction:

You know Burroughs & Chapin [Burroughs & Collins at the time] *was a big deal in those days. They ran everything, including the city council, and if any zoning or reconstruction was done or not they were the ones who*

Barbara Horner's family beach cottage on Seventy-sixth Avenue North was torn down to build a resort. *Barbara Horner collection.*

did it, and they kept it very, very secretive. So about '75 we found out that this whole block had been rezoned commercial. No one had a public hearing; no one said anything. Nothing. So we realized something was going on that we didn't have any control over, and so they wouldn't even talk to me. They just said, "No, it's done. It's all zoned commercial." So by…'79 and '80, then they began to land on me…It was a lovely old street…wooden beach houses–type stuff. And they all sold out, and they were all torn down and thrown away. Except for me. [I] *had to hold out three years…They came to me, and they said, "We will give you this amount of money—Get out."* And I said, *"No."* That was one year. [The next year, they said], *"OK, we'll give you this amount of money, and we will move your house." That was year two.* I said, *"No, no, no, no." Year three,* [they said], *"We will give you this amount of money, and we will find you a lot somewhere in town and move your house to it." Four years. By '83, I was realizing they had torn down the whole block except for my house, and everybody was older, my father's age, in their seventies and eighties. And they just sold out and moved out. And so I said, "I'm going to stay, even though you're tearing down all around me, I'm staying." And they said, "OK, here's the deal. We have a lot we will give you free and build you a house to your specifications on that lot, and give you X amount of dollars."*

45

Finally, Horner accepted the offer. Her new house was built a few blocks south of Seventy-sixth Avenue North and a few doors away from the ocean, and per her request, it is an almost exact replica of the home she sold to the developer. A high-rise condo-tel constructed after she moved there obscures her ocean view. She still feels resentment about what happened to that block on Seventy-sixth Avenue North now occupied by Carolina Winds Oceanfront Resort and said, "I have a, I guess you'd say an almost permanent anger about this because I'm a tree person, and I like forests. And they literally, you know, tore down all the forest up there."

5

SPENDING THE NIGHT

Before the train started taking passengers to the beach in 1900 and before the Seaside Inn opened in 1901, many modern beach visitors arrived on foot, which was called traveling by "shank's mare." Others rode horses or used horse-drawn carts, buggies and stagecoaches, and farm livestock like donkeys, mules and oxen were sometimes drafted into transportation service.

Depending on where they were coming from, it could take a while to get to the beach. Camping along the way was the norm, and as those early beachgoers gathered around nighttime campfires while traveling through swampy forests, they heard cougars scream, coyotes howl and bull alligators roar. A 1920s photo of Myrtle Beach campers shows a man in a dark suit and wearing a white collared shirt and hat sitting on the ground in front of a swash or inlet. Beside him are three women sitting on the ground in front of a simple triangular canvas tent and wearing full long skirts, long-sleeved high-neck blouses and wide-brim hats. Visible inside the tent are a table covered in mosquito netting and a small armless rocking chair.

Eventually, automobiles and roads on which to drive them were in use to get to the beach, but people still liked camping. For a long time, camping was free, and travelers looked for pleasant spots to pitch tents. But soon, landowners decided too many travelers were trespassing and leaving messes, but many restaurant owners recognized potential customers and offered free camping on their properties. In the Myrtle Beach area, people camped on the beach long after there were boardinghouses, motor courts, motels and

Early camping trips to Myrtle Beach meant bringing tents, food and furniture, often by horse and cart. *Horry County Museum, Conway, South Carolina.*

hotels, but local ordinances finally banished the practice. However, today, Myrtle Beach remains a favorite East Coast camping spot with several large oceanfront campgrounds.

BOARDINGHOUSES

The next step up in comfort, at least from a four-walls-and-roof perspective, came in the form of people leasing out rooms in their homes.

Boardinghouses, sometimes called guesthouses, were popular through the 1960s in Myrtle Beach. A 1953 brochure entitled "Myrtle Beach, South Carolina, Accommodations and Conveniences" includes information about the Miramar-Reinhart, an oceanfront home on the north end of town in a "preferred resort section" that boasted of a "homelike atmosphere" where "all rooms are large and comfortable with Simmons Beautyrest beds. First-floor bedrooms available. Private or connecting baths. Two spacious living

The Wee Blu Inn was a homelike oceanfront boardinghouse. *Author's collection.*

rooms, cool and restful porches, beach house, and hot and cold showers for bathers. A bountiful and delicious breakfast served from 8 to 10:30 A.M." It had gaily striped window awnings and a curving exterior staircase leading to a second-floor porch.

The Murphy's was at 2300 North Ocean Boulevard, where there are now high-rise hotels. It had two oceanfront buildings: one in front that looked like an old beach cottage with an umbrella roof and wraparound porch, and a long two-story structure behind it with sixteen rooms that had "either private or connecting baths." Operators Mr. and Mrs. A.E. Murphy offered meals on the "American Plan—Three Meals Daily, Two on Sunday."

The Belvedere also offered the American plan, and its advertisement boasted of "home-made pastries and desserts." Located at 1903 North Ocean Boulevard, where Lulu's Café now operates, it cost $5.00–$6.00 per day to stay there during the summer of 1953. In the off-season, a room and meal package went for $4.50.

Barbara Horner remembers the Periscope Cottage off present-day Mr. Joe White Avenue, where there is now a farmers' market. The John Singleton family owned it. "It was not advertised or anything," Horner said, "but people knew it was a local boardinghouse that they could come and stay [at] for a week at the beach...Oh yeah, that whole block was torn down, and it was typical of a beach—what they called boardinghouses, where people would board for a week and have their meals and everything there."

Many remaining boardinghouses are being removed to make way for new and taller structures, even though local preservationists agree they

The Periscope was a boardinghouse owned by the John Singleton family. It was located off Mr. Joe White Avenue. *Barbara Horner collection.*

should be protected. One guesthouse that survives (although now it is apartments) is Moose's Guest House at 307 North Ocean Boulevard, and its appearance is almost exactly the same as it was in 1953. It even has the same pink stucco.

MOTOR COURTS

Motor courts were also a big step up from camping. They used to "line the highways in Myrtle Beach…Evolved from tent sites along highways that matured into small cabins tightly placed on a small lot in urban areas, the motor court was usually U or L shaped, much like later motels, and had a prominent office building in the front, facing the road, often with an inviting, unique theme."

Barbara Stokes wrote that the first lodging to be labeled a motor court was the Ocean Pines Motor Court located at 3801 North Kings Highway, which opened in March 1940 under the ownership and management of Nordyke Metzger and George Olson. A black-and-white postcard depicting an artistic rendering of the building says on the back, "In restricted residential section, 2 miles North of business section. Every room has twin beds, private bath, and private entrance. Completely new building and furnishings." As

The Ocean Pines Motor Court had twin beds in every room. *Author's collection.*

Noel Court at 306 Sixth Avenue South is one of two remaining historic motor courts in Myrtle Beach. *Photo by Becky Billingsley.*

of the spring of 2014, Spyglass Adventure Golf is at the former Ocean Pines Motor Court site.

In 1953, rooms at Parker's Motor Hotel at Seventeenth Avenue North had private tile baths with showers and tubs. During the summer, electric fans were provided, and in the winter, guests could control heat with their own thermostats. T&C. Motor Courts was located "four blocks south of [the] business section" and one block from the ocean. Its fifty rooms were laid out in a series of apartments that looked like tiny houses. Some apartments had their own kitchens, while others were more like hotel rooms. However, they all had their own bathrooms and air conditioning.

When the Horry County Historic Resources Survey was published in 2009, two motor courts remained: Smith Motor Court at 204 U.S. 17 Business South and Noel Motor Court at 306 Sixth Avenue South. As of the spring of 2014, they both are still operating, although Smith's was renamed Ocean West Motel.

Pre–World War II Hotels

The Seaside Inn was the first hotel in Myrtle Beach, and it opened on May 23, 1901, with rates of two dollars per day, which included three meals. By 1921, it had added twenty-five rooms.

By 1911, its name had changed to the Sea Side Hotel (also called the Seaside Inn). An advertisement in a North Carolina newspaper said:

> *This well known hotel having been refitted and refurnished, located on one of the finest beaches on the South Atlantic Coast is ready for the Summer resorter. It appeals strongly to those wanting a sea side vacation, excellent surf bathing, boating, fishing, etc. Music and Dancing at the Pavilion. Absolutely no malaria in this region, the sandy soil thoroughly draining the surrounding country. We desire to cater to the best families, those wanting all the comforts of home life. The summer schedule of trains to and from Myrtle Beach enables one to leave any part of Eastern South Carolina and reach Myrtle Beach for noon dinner. Special Rates by the Week for Families and Children. St. John & Son, Myrtle Beach, South Carolina.*

The allure of Myrtle Beach was reported that summer in a Lumberton, North Carolina newspaper column: "Quite a large crowd took advantage

With the opening of the Seaside Inn in 1901, tourists could spend beach vacations in relative comfort. *Horry County Museum, Conway, South Carolina.*

of the new summer rates in Myrtle Beach and spent last Sunday there. They report a beautiful beach, good comfortable hotel with splendid fare and recommend all their friends who want to rest in the fresh breezes to go there."

A 1926 advertisement in the *Florence Morning News* from the Myrtle Beach Sales Company (which had district sales offices in Greenville, Columbia, Florence, Charlotte and Winston-Salem) promoted a Governor's Ball and formal Thanksgiving opening at the "New Year-'Round Seaside Inn and

Above: The Ocean Plaza Fishing Pier was at Fourteenth Avenue North. *Author's collection.*

Left: Lafayette Manor was built in 1926 and was located on Ninth Avenue North until it was torn down in 1960 to make room for a parking lot. *Author's collection.*

the New Restricted Golf Club Section." The event, held November 25–27, had South Carolina governor Thomas McLeod in attendance. There were deer and foxhunts each morning, and "Brig. Gen. Bowley With His Camp Bragg Band" performed. The Seaside Inn's two dining rooms were the sites for "Special Thanksgiving turkey dinners, barbecues [and] plenty of sea food."

The Seaside Inn was moved a short distance away from the Myrtle Beach Pavilion site, turned sideways and renamed the Strand Hotel in 1927. It was torn down in 1949.

The Yacht Club and Fishing Pier was built at Fourteenth Avenue North in 1922, and later, Sam Gardner, who renamed it the Ocean Plaza Hotel, bought it. It was an imposing structure and the largest on the beach at the time with its two stories, and its pier had a casino. In 1971, the hotel was replaced by Myrtle Beach's first high-rise hotel, called the Yachtsman, and the pier is now Fourteenth Avenue Pier.

Near the Seaside Inn, Lafayette Manor opened in 1926 on Ninth Avenue North. "It had indoor plumbing and electricity, a first for the town," a note in the December 8, 1999 *Sun News* says. "Its large dining room was a popular place for meetings, dinners and wedding receptions." John T. Woodside and his brothers, who also built the Ocean Forest Hotel, built Lafayette Manor and originally used it as a real estate sales office and administration building. It was torn down in 1960 to make way for a parking lot.

By the 1930s, there were enough lodging establishments to say the city had a "Hotel Section," according to the Myrtle Beach Comprehensive Plan:

Evidence of the re-emergence of the Myrtle Beach Farms Company as a significant player in real estate development is provided by a set of maps and plats, prepared for Myrtle Beach farms in the 1930s that trace the opening of sections to the north. The first of these is a 1933 map of Myrtle Beach prepared for the Myrtle Beach Farms Company compiling information from previous surveys and combining it with additions and changes. It included all the area referred to as the Hotel Section, bounded to the north by 9th Avenue North, and extended from 9th Avenue North to 40th Avenue North, including all the land situated between the ocean and Kings Highway.

An example of new erasing the old is the story of Patricia Forester Rousseau Boyd (1899–1999), who, as a young woman in 1934, moved from North Wilkesboro, North Carolina, to Myrtle Beach. She founded the Patricia Court off Ocean Boulevard at Twenty-eighth Avenue North, and in 1941, it was joined by the Patricia Inn, which had 102 rooms.

"The three-story inn is an odd mixture of styles," a 1985 newspaper article said. "The exterior is a massive square, white frame structure with green and white awnings. Columns run along the beachside patio. The lobby and dining room are spacious, detailed with intricate molding and

Above: The Robert and Patricia Boyd estate was a large plot of acreage between Ocean Boulevard and Kings Highway. The house was razed and the land is being developed in 2014. *Barbara Horner collection.*

Left: Myrtle Lodge was torn down in 1969 for an expansion of the pavilion. *Author's collection.*

columns. Those who have long frequented the inn remember when men and boys wore coats and ties to dinner and women wore long evening frocks."

Hurricane Hazel caused damage in 1954, but the buildings were repaired and remodeled. Patricia married Robert W. Boyd, who operated laundry services for hotels. In the late 1970s, Patricia Boyd and a partner sold the

Patricia Inn. In 1985, those owners sold the property to developers who demolished the inn, and in 1988, the Patricia Grand Resort Hotel opened. It is an eighteen-story-high complex of four buildings with 308 rooms and indoor and outdoor pools.

The Boyds lived in a brick columned mansion facing Ocean Boulevard in the Ocean Forest area of Myrtle Beach. The gently rolling lawn studded with trees encompassed several acres, and the property extended from Kings Highway to Ocean Boulevard. As of 2013, the mansion was torn down, and in 2014, the property was being developed.

Myrtle Lodge was built in 1939 at 406 Eighth Avenue North. The three-story brick building was torn down in 1969 to make room for expansion of the pavilion amusement park.

By 1940, the Hotel Section was "extensively developed" from between the ocean and Chester Street, and the oceanfront was

> *almost one hundred percent developed north of the Hotel Section 9th Avenue North to around 45th Avenue North. The second row from 9th Avenue North to approximately 29th or 30th Avenues North was also one hundred percent developed…The oceanfront and second row development were almost exclusively residential in scale. Boarding houses and guesthouses were common south of 31st Avenue North along Ocean Boulevard and in the downtown and Hotel Section.*

THE CHESTERFIELD INN

The Chesterfield Inn had earlier incarnations, but the one that lasted was a building constructed in 1946. Literature from the South Carolina Department of Archives and History says it was "significant for its association with Myrtle Beach's period of growth and prosperity as a coastal community resort from 1926 to 1954; as an excellent representative example of the motels/hotels commonly built in Myrtle Beach in the mid-twentieth century; and as an unusual example of Colonial Revival style architecture in the Myrtle Beach area…The 1946 building is of frame construction with a brick veneer exterior. It has a rectangular plan, end to front gable roof, and a raised basement foundation."

The same family operated the Chesterfield, built by Steven Chapman of Chesterfield, South Carolina, for more than fifty years. The property was added to the National Register of Historic Places in 1996, and two families

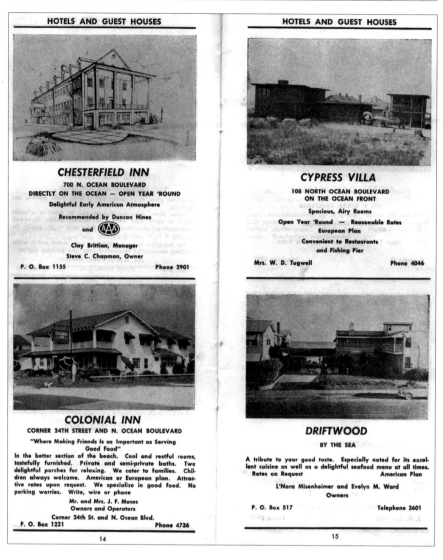

HOTELS AND GUEST HOUSES

CHESTERFIELD INN

700 N. OCEAN BOULEVARD
DIRECTLY ON THE OCEAN — OPEN YEAR 'ROUND

Delightful Early American Atmosphere

Recommended by Duncan Hines

and (AAA)

Clay Brittian, Manager
Steve C. Chapman, Owner

P. O. Box 1155   Phone 2901

COLONIAL INN

CORNER 24TH STREET AND N. OCEAN BOULEVARD

"Where Making Friends Is as Important as Serving Good Food"

In the better section of the beach. Cool and restful rooms, tastefully furnished. Private and semi-private baths. Two delightful porches for relaxing. We cater to families. Children always welcome. American or European plan. Attractive rates upon request. We specialize in good food. No parking worries. Write, wire or phone

Mr. and Mrs. J. F. Moses
Owners and Operators

Corner 24th St. and N. Ocean Blvd.
P. O. Box 1221   Phone 4736

14

HOTELS AND GUEST HOUSES

CYPRESS VILLA

108 NORTH OCEAN BOULEVARD
ON THE OCEAN FRONT

Spacious, Airy Rooms

Open Year 'Round — Reasonable Rates
European Plan

Convenient to Restaurants
and Fishing Pier

Mrs. W. D. Tugwell   Phone 4046

DRIFTWOOD

BY THE SEA

A tribute to your good taste. Especially noted for its excellent cuisine as well as a delightful seafood menu at all times. Rates on Request   American Plan

L'Nora Misenheimer and Evelyn M. Ward
Owners

P. O. Box 517   Telephone 3601

15

Its placement on the National Register of Historic Places did not save the Chesterfield Inn from being razed in 2012. *Author's collection.*

bought the Chesterfield in 2004. On August 22, 2012, the Chesterfield Inn was razed. In its place is a mini golf course.

Many locals questioned why the Chesterfield Inn wasn't preserved since it was on the National Register of Historic Places, and the answer is the NRHP doesn't protect properties if the municipality in which it is located doesn't have any historic preservation ordinances.

In February 2014, City of Myrtle Beach planning director Jack Walker confirmed the city does not have historic preservation ordinances or a board overseeing historic preservation. "The comprehensive plan for the city recommends that we take actions to preserve our heritage, including establishing necessary boards/commissions working with neighborhood organizations to develop ordinances that encourage protection of cultural resources and the establishment of protective measures to preserve our natural resources," he said.

In its comprehensive plan, the city of Myrtle Beach has listed sixty-three properties that are either on the NRHP or are considered historically or archaeologically significant. Regarding historic preservation, the plan says:

> *Since the heady days of the 1920s, expansion has been the major means by which Myrtle Beach accommodated economic development. However, redevelopment has also been used here. Local businessmen have redeveloped their properties as changes in the accommodations and amusements industries required new and larger facilities. Major disasters (such as Hurricane Hazel in 1954), and changes in financing (such as the National Flood Insurance Program in 1978 which provided affordable flood protection for beachfront property owners), and changes in marketing (such as the designation of Myrtle Beach as a metropolitan area after the 1990 census, which meant the federal government would begin distributing more demographic information about the area to national investors) have provided their own impetus for redevelopment through the years. All of this, combined with the native desire to eliminate the area's isolation and improve its chances for participating in the economic mainstream, has meant that many of the buildings that made Myrtle Beach's history do not survive today. All of this also means that many residents have not demanded preservation of what is left of the area's architectural heritage.*

Horry County has a board of architectural review that can make recommendations for historic preservation of the county's some two hundred properties on the Horry County Historic Property Register, but without any backup from local preservation ordinances, Myrtle Beach historic properties can be torn down if the owner wishes.

"The Chesterfield was only listed on the National Register," Horry County senior planner Adam Emrick, said in February 2014. "It was located within the municipal limits of the city of Myrtle Beach and therefore subject to [the city's] zoning laws. Myrtle Beach has no historic preservation component to [its] zoning ordinance, and we're not statutorily equipped to prevent the demolition of the Chesterfield. It was a major loss to the historic fabric of the community."

POPULUXE MOTELS

After World War II, and especially after Hurricane Hazel destroyed many old buildings in 1954, a futuristic style of motel design called Populuxe (*popular* + *luxury*) became the vogue. Architecture and design writer Thomas

Midtown Motel is an example of Populuxe architecture with decorative concrete block walls. *Photo by Becky Billingsley.*

Hine coined the term Populuxe as the title of his first book, and style features include concrete block "curtains," or walls, on the street, bright colors, flat roofs and iconic retro signage. Populuxe designs were also prevalent in automobiles, home décor, toys and more.

While the Populuxe period started in the late 1940s, most examples in Myrtle Beach date from 1955 through 1970, according to the 2009 Horry County Historic Resources Survey, which also refers to motels of this period as "recent past architecture":

> *Horry County holds perhaps the best collection of recent past architecture in the state, as its boom period for residential and tourism growth occurred in the 1950s, spurring the construction of hundreds of new structures…Recent past architecture is just now coming of age and into serious study by the historic preservation field, and yet the attention is outpaced by the demolition of buildings from the mid twentieth century. This is especially true in Myrtle Beach, which houses the highest number of midcentury motels on the county's coast, if not the state's coast. However, modern resort development consumes blocks of oceanfront property in Myrtle Beach and small motels fall to the wrecking ball at a rapid pace.*

Problems facing the Populuxe motels are higher taxes due to rising land costs and competing with nearby newer high-rise motels with more luxurious amenities. Given the choice of spending money to upgrade or selling out to someone who wants to tear down the old motel and build a new high-rise, many motel owners opt to sell out. The survey says:

> *Much of the current dilemma for Populuxe motels can be traced to two problems, zoning and lack of preservation ordinances. The zoning in place allows for high-rise hotels of more than 200 feet, with more concessions in height if certain requirements are met along the ground floor to make it appealing for pedestrian traffic. Such zoning clearly favors large developers and resorts, and dismisses the eclectic building heights in Myrtle Beach, which range from one to seven stories for homes and hotels built until the early 1970s.*

Forty-eight Populuxe motels the 2009 survey recommended for preservation include the Rainbow Court Hotel at 411 North Ocean Boulevard, Waikiki Village Motel at 1500 South Ocean Boulevard,

Waikiki Village is a Populuxe Motel surrounded by modern high-rises. *Photo by Becky Billingsley.*

Bermuda Sands Resort at 104 North Ocean Boulevard, the Wayfarer Motel at 311 North Ocean Boulevard and the Sea Nymph Motel at 601 North Ocean Boulevard. The Beverly Motel at 703 North Ocean Boulevard and the Mid-Town Motor Inn at 309 Eighth Avenue North are included in a list of Populuxe motels created by Katherine Fuller, whose 2002 dissertation for the Goucher College Master of Arts in Historic Preservation is about the preservation of Populuxe motels in Myrtle Beach and the Wildwoods in New Jersey. The Beverly was torn down in early 2013, and as of the spring of 2014, the Mid-Town was not open.

Not saving these Populuxe structures, the survey says, would be to ignore a demographic of customers who seek local history: "They need to be recognized as the tourist draw they historically have been, currently are, and could be in the future. The city and county need to capitalize on their unique architecture and size for marketing, and should move quickly to preserve them, as they are in imminent danger of demolition for new developments."

MOTOR COURTS

MONTICELLO MOTOR LODGE

U. S. 17 AT 19TH AND 20TH AVENUES

The newest motor lodge in Myrtle Beach. Sixteen cross-ventilated rooms. Some air-conditioned. Forced air heat for cool nights. Every room has private tile bath with shower.

Mr. and Mrs. Peter Fields, Owners

Mrs. Thomas Tuck, Manager   Phone 6291

OCEAN PINES MOTOR COURT

HIGHWAY 17, 1½ MILES NORTH OF TOWN

Located one block from ocean in attractively landscaped pine grove. 35 well-appointed hotel rooms with Beautyrest beds, private tile baths and cross ventilation. Each room equipped with radio. Nine completely furnished housekeeping units, electrically equipped, ranging in size from efficiency to four rooms. Steam heated. Restaurant 400 feet. Select clientele, quiet and restful.

Spacious new central office and community house.
Recommended by AAA, Duncan Hines and Quality Courts
Nash and Carey Talbot, Managers
Rates on Request   Phone 3691

30

MOTOR COURTS

PALMETTO MOTOR COURT

MYRTLE BEACH, S. C.

One mile north of business district and only one block from the ocean. A new court offering all the conveniences for the traveling public—steam heat, Beautyrest and Airfoam double or twin beds—efficiency apartments. AAA approved. Member Courtesy Courts United, Inc.

Mr. and Mrs. J. C. Lathan, Owners-Operators

Rates on Request   Phone 5546

THE PALMS MOTOR COURT

TWO MILES NORTH OF BUSINESS DISTRICT ON U. S. 17

In the quiet, restful district of Myrtle Beach—only one block from the beach. Modern rooms to accommodate from one to six each have private tile baths, air conditioning, and steam heat. Spacious landscaped grounds provide recreational facilities including shuffleboard, croquet, and horseshoe pitching. Golf, fishing, and tennis nearby.

Recommended by AAA and Ocean Hiway Association

AAA Restaurant Adjoining

Bob Jones and Bob Hasty, Owners-Operators

Rates on Request   Phone 4846

31

Motor courts were common in the 1940s and '50s. Author's collection.

LOOKING AHEAD TO SAVE THE PAST

Myrtle Beach city planners work at the direction of city council members and the city manager, and if they don't indicate that forming a historic preservation committee or historic preservation ordinances are priorities, then the city's eight employees in the planning department have to focus on other projects. As of the spring of 2014, neither the city manager nor council members have asked for a committee or ordinances to ensure the preservation of historic properties within Myrtle Beach, but forming a historic preservation committee is on the city's list of short-term goals to achieve within the next five years.

On a case-by-case basis, city of Myrtle Beach planners have worked hard to ensure history is preserved in many ways. The survey recommends instituting tax relief, grants and low- or no interest loans to help these structures remain intact.

6

THE OCEAN FOREST HOTEL

The Ocean Forest Hotel was considered one of most beautiful and upscale hotels on the East Coast. In 1926, John T. Woodside and his brothers, who were from Greenville, South Carolina, bought 64,488 acres of land from Myrtle Beach Farms Co. for $950,000. The Woodsides planned to built a resort that would attract wealthy northerners. The hotel, which opened in 1930, changed Myrtle Beach from a quaint seaside getaway to a world-class resort.

In January 1926, the *Florence Morning News* teased its readers with a three-inch bold capitalized headline reading, "Myrtle Beach Development on Mammoth Scale," with a sub-headline that said, "Piedmont Capitalists Will Announce Full Plans Soon; Conway Shows Excitement." A few months later, another article in the same paper told of the Woodsides' Myrtle Beach development plans, saying:

> *The press on every hand has greeted with approval and great delight and expression of confidence, the announcement of the purchase of Myrtle Beach by the Woodsides and their elaborate program of development...It is interesting to note that in their program covering the development of the resort they are determined to get as far away from the loud, noisy, unattractive, unconventional, undignified form that resort centers so frequently take.*

A 1929 article in the *Aiken Standard* told of the Ocean Forest Hotel as it was in the final stages of construction. "New $1,500,000 Hotel to Open at

Construction on the Ocean Forest Hotel was ongoing in 1929. *Horry County Museum, Conway, South Carolina.*

Myrtle Beach Early in December," the page-five headline says, calling the event "an opening of unusual interest." It mentions that the week before the October 25 article was published, the hotel's opening was announced by project architect R.O. Brannan of Johnson and Brannon in New York. The Myrtle Beach area is described as "104 square miles of virgin forests, rich farm lands and picturesque dunes. Great forests are separated from the water only by sand dunes, myrtle and other small growth."

A city of Myrtle Beach Comprehensive Plan, updated in 2011, says, "The Woodside family was captivated by the area's natural beauty and planned a development that was attractive in its own right. The combination of the natural and built environments was an important business strategy and was highlighted in advertising for the new resort."

The area around the Ocean Forest had "nine beautiful fresh water lakes in the woods near the ocean" that the 1929 article says were going to be used as part of a hunting game preserve. It also mentions the Ocean Forest Golf Club, which had "its own lobby, lounging rooms, card rooms, dining rooms, grill room, lockers and bed rooms." As for the hotel, it was described as being

of the modern sky-scraper type, of steel and concrete structure and elegantly appointed with 225 rooms and bath...The building of the hotel and *development of the Myrtle Beach area are looked upon as being one of the most outstanding and significant enterprises in the south. The Myrtle Beach Estates have been incorporated for $6,000,000, and the holdings have an approximate value of more than $10,000,000.*

The City of Myrtle Beach established an Ocean Forest Memorial Park, and its literature about the Ocean Forest says:

The center of Woodside's vision was a Miami-style high-rise hotel. Built on the ocean-side surrounded by pines and myrtle bushes that lined the shore, the grand white structure earned its name the Ocean Forest Hotel. The Ocean Forest Hotel formally opened its doors Friday evening, February 21, 1930. The hotel, standing 29 feet above sea level, with a 10-story wedding cake tower with two 5-story wings…had gardens, pools, stables…on thirteen acres. Some of the amenities were marble stairways, Czechoslovakian crystal chandeliers, Grecian columns, faucets that dispensed salt water to the 202 ventilated bathrooms, oriental rugs in the marble floored lobby [and a] grand ballroom. Guests lingered in the luxurious surroundings, playing shuffleboard on the hotel lawn, splashing in the surf, dancing to big-name bands, and dining on superb cuisine. The Ocean Forest had a corps of uniformed bellmen who would tote a guest's suitcase to his or her room. A carpeted double stairway flanked the ground floor entrance, and led guests through a columned portico onto the second floor. Eleven stories up, a beacon topped a graceful cupola. Old-fashioned deck chairs lined the hotel porches, and professional landscaping enhanced the hotel's campus. [A] spacious lobby, bedecked with fancy furniture, the dining room was decorated with a kind of gilt-looking wallpaper and lit by rows of polished chandeliers. Awaiting patrons were countless tables covered in white tablecloths, silverware rolled in linen napkins, and centerpieces of fresh flowers.

Timing was not on the Woodsides' side, because the financial crash of 1929 happened just a few months before the Ocean Forest Hotel opened. The wealthy people the hotel was supposed to cater to were hurting financially. John Woodside had even grander plans to develop a sixteen-thousand-acre high-end resort called Arcady, and toward that goal, he also built the Ocean Forest Golf Course and Country Club, which still exists and is now known as Pine Lakes Country Club. Plans for Arcady included "paved roads, utilities, a yacht basin, polo grounds and bridle paths," the

The Ocean Forest Hotel was completed in 1930. This postcard was published by Delta Drug Co. in Myrtle Beach. *Author's collection.*

Myrtle Beach Comprehensive Plan says, and was described by the Woodside brothers as "a national playground where the leaders of contemporary life may sustain their capacity for work by bringing to its utmost the art of rest and recreation." However, the Great Depression negatively affected the financial health of the Ocean Forest and its owners, and the Woodsides were not able to make payments on the land they bought. They sold some of it, but in 1933, "the remainder reverted to Myrtle Beach Farms, which would play a significant part in the town's growth."

After that, the Ocean Forest Hotel had several different owners. A 1935 advertisement in the Lumberton, North Carolina *Robesonian* newspaper listed "Messrs. Littlegreen & Lynch" as the hotel's "leasers and managers," and an article in the same newspaper dated June 3, 1935, says that 1935 was the men's third season operating the Ocean Forest. The article continues:

> *For a time it seemed as though no one wanted to take over the place, but Messrs. Littlegreen and Lynch decided in 1933 to take over the hotel and gamble on its being a success. The gamble, however, has been won, due not to pure luck, but more to able, efficient and engagable management...The Ocean Forest typifies the spirit of Myrtle Beach more than any other one single factor and it is decidedly the premier attraction of Ocean Forest, a highly restricted residential area. It is situated about three miles north of Myrtle Beach*

proper and as the center of a splendidly executed plan presenting a network of boulevards, avenues, drives and bridle paths. The hotel immediately faces the strand, which has become a private bathing beach for guests of the hotel and residents of the area of Ocean Forest.

A 1935 advertisement announced the hotel's formal opening for the summer season on May 31 and describes its amenities as including

a modern fire-proof building, 11 stories high with 220 guest rooms, each with private baths, running fresh water and some with salt water baths, all tastefully and beautifully furnished. Dine here in one of the world's most beautiful dining rooms. Luncheon and dinner music by a nationally known Palm Beach orchestra. A renowned southern chef provides seafood and southern dishes that tempt both the eye and appetite. Surf-bathing, sun bathing, fishing, golf, archery, trap shooting, tennis and various other forms of out door recreation.

Also in 1935, the hotel's owners held an essay contest in response to the question, "Why Myrtle Beach is the Ideal Spot for a Vacation and the Ocean Forest Hotel the Best Place to Stay." The winner was R.E. Haynes, who resided at 230 Park Avenue in New York City. He won a week's stay for two, complete with meals. The winning essay reads:

Whether on a short or long vacation, beautiful Myrtle Beach is most ideally situated with good roads leading in from all points and adequate transportation, making it easily accessible. It is well termed "America's Finest Strand" with its smooth, wide beach, and destined to become a great mid-south resort. The justly named "Unspoiled Playground" and development at the beach and the people enjoying it lend an air of permanence so often lacking at seaside resorts. This, of course, brings us to talk about the Ocean Forest hotel at the north end of the beach. This magnificent structure, that cost a million and looks it, excels in comfort and service at surprisingly small cost. The salt air gives on a sharp appetite, which is well taken care of when you stay at the Ocean Forest. Besides music and dancing, there are many advantages in connection with the hotel, one of which is the excellent golf course adjoining. The setting for this course among the tall pines is unique and its well kept greens and fairways are a joy to "duffer" or "pro." Couple all these things with the immediately surrounding picturesque and historic country along the Carolina coast and you really wonder why anyone goes anywhere but to Myrtle Beach and the Ocean Forest hotel for a complete vacation.

A 1952 advertisement for the Ocean Forest lists its rates. A single room started at $14 per day, a double was $20 and a suite was priced at $30. A "modified American" meal plan was available that included morning and evening meals. Amenities that year included surf bathing, golf, tennis, beach sports, clock golf, shuffleboard, volleyball, horseback riding, fishing, sightseeing and "dancing nightly beneath the stars at the beautiful Ocean Forest Marine Patio." The average family income in 1952 was $3,900, or $75 per week.

In the early 1950s, when Ann Vereen was about nine or ten years old, she had a friend whose aunt and uncle had a home near the Ocean Forest. "We'd walk to the Ocean Forest Hotel," she said. "We went in and played in the ballroom and where the pool was, and nobody cared. It was a great playground. The ballroom was large and beautiful. I remember chandeliers. I thought it was just a grand place because I was born in Horry County over near Conway, and when we'd go over there and play, it was like New York City. It was like a castle; it was so wonderful."

Beyond being a place for tourists to stay, the Ocean Forest Hotel was big enough to host conventions. Its grandeur and oceanfront location made it attractive for hundreds of organizations looking for beach fun with their seminars. In June 1955, 450 members and guests of the Bakers Association of the Carolinas had a three-day convention that started with a "get-together party," an article in the *Florence Morning News* says. The second night they saw a troupe called Carolina Showboat, which performed *El Rancho Grande*, described as "a Western production flavored with cowboys and Indians, and spiced with a bit of Mexico."

Locals and visitors used the hotel for private events like weddings, proms and parties, and public events such as ticketed concerts and plays were held there as well as activities for the annual June Sun Fun Festival. In 1956, a Charleston, West Virginia *Gazette* article says the Ocean Forest Marine Patio was the site of the Sun Fun Masqueraders Ball, "a colorful panorama of vivid costumes as members and guests compete for handsome gifts. Crowds of spectators will gather at the patio entrance to see the unusual costumes of the Masqueraders."

In 1968, management applied for a building permit to add twenty-eight guest rooms and two meeting rooms. The expansion cost was listed as $156,000.

JoAnne Utterback worked in the coffee shop at the Ocean Forest in the summers of 1967 and '68, when she was seventeen and eighteen years old. The first summer, she and a girlfriend lived in the "Bull Pen," located behind

"Private swimming pool is one of the many attractions that make this a convention center," this Ocean Forest Hotel postcard says. *Author's collection.*

the hotel. "It was circular," she said. "When the people came to town and they had to come by horse and they brought their servants, they had to have places to park the horses and carts and have the servants stay. They could walk the horses on the circle in front of the Bull Pen. Underneath is where they parked the horses and cars, and up top was where the help slept." The guests' servants' accommodations were used as summer employees' housing during later years, and Utterback recalls her tiny space having room for two cots and a sink, and there was a separate tiny bathroom with a toilet.

Utterback also recalls something else for which the Ocean Forest became known: prostitution. "I'm sitting in the coffee shop with people, and there's this one woman with…cleavage that went almost up to her Adam's apple. I'd never seen anything like it before. Later, when she left, they told me she lived down the street in a little home that rents rooms, and she was a prostitute. All the prostitutes had to come in a little back door and have to be escorted up, and it was kind of run by the doorman."

With little notice to local residents, the Ocean Forest Hotel was demolished in 1974 after it was determined it was more cost effective to build something new there instead of spending money to upgrade the existing structure. Today, modern vacation lodging stands in place of the Ocean Forest Hotel, but its traffic circle entrance is still a terminus for several streets that radiate from it. That circle was part of an important design element for the hotel.

"People remember the Ocean Forest as a grand hotel," the city of Myrtle Beach 2011 Comprehensive Plan says. The plan continues:

> *Perhaps more grand than its architecture was its carefully crafted place in the landscape. Two diagonal streets, Poinsett and Calhoun, cut dramatically across the grain of nearby streets to focus on the spot where the hotel once stood. The developers made a conscious decision to include a very subtle feature to this arrangement: the width of the pavement of the two streets increases to emphasize the hotel's visual importance. Along the two diagonal streets, two landscaped islands were planned to interrupt Kings Highway (US 17 Business) to slow traffic and announce the presence of the residential neighborhood. These are three design features whose only purpose was to heighten the visual effect and improve the aesthetics of the development. Unfortunately, the landscaped islands were removed to accommodate vehicular traffic and the buildings that replaced the Ocean Forest were not designed to take advantage of the very special stage that had been created for the hotel.*

Karon Bowers Jones lived in Myrtle Beach during her childhood, and she remembers her father, Jimmy Bowers, shooting off fireworks from the hotel's roof in his role as hotel employee. Many local high schools held proms at the Ocean Forest, and Jones's graduating class of 1974 was the last to have a senior prom there.

The Ocean Forest Hotel was designed to make a strong visual statement when approached from the west. *Author's collection.*

When Jones learned the hotel was torn down, she said:

> *There were a lot of emotions I guess going on…I remember as a youngster driving, when I first got my license, going around—you know it had a circular driveway in the front, so when you came down the street you had to go around it…and I remember I was just going around and around the fountain in the middle. And then there were horse stables that were in front of, farther up in front of the Ocean Forest Hotel. So to me, it was a landmark, which I think* [it was to everybody]. *And* [what] *I think it was* [is that] *you want to keep old things around, but times are changing. And we never see things that we used to grow up with. They're just not there anymore. It was big. I can still see it looked like a big castle. As a small child, that's exactly what it looked like, a huge castle.*

Ann Vereen says she wishes she "had more foresight then to have kept them from [tearing it down]. I probably couldn't have, but we could have formed a group. I had no idea really it was being done. It just happened, and it was just devastating that they tore that down."

"We go to other places, and we pay great money to see these castles and great homes that other people had," Joyce Herian said. "It would have been just so fabulous to have had that here, but the owners probably saw the potential of that land and what it could make for them…People were not as conscientious then as they are now about preserving yesteryear for the future."

"The rooms were small, and they had these nice big rooms on the boulevard. Nobody really wanted to stay there," Joyce Herian's son, Jack Bourne, said. "A lot of people didn't know about [the demolition] beforehand, because they were worried about people getting in an uproar over it or something like that. But they used to pipe salt water into the building, and all the pipes couldn't handle that salt water. It would have cost them a lot of money to bring it up, keep it maintained."

"Inside, it was nice," Ed Herian said. "I'm still disgusted that they didn't leave that as a landmark of Myrtle Beach. Now they've got a piece of junk up there."

The Horry County Board of Architectural Review considers several homes near the Ocean Forest site that are circa 1930–1950 to be historic, and its members would like to see it be made an official historic district. However, there is concern they won't be preserved:

A well-preserved residential community, this area retains integrity of location, design, setting, materials, workmanship, feeling and association. Very little alterations or infill mar the proposed district, and it is one of the best collections of fine homes in the county...Much of the modern commercial development and high-rise motels along the ocean have replaced historic beach homes, some of them cleared away by the natural disaster of Hurricane Hazel, but many of them victims of encroaching development. Mid-century commercial buildings face the same threat today, as their older facades compete for tourist dollars with brand new facilities along the Highway 17 Bypass, and their land is coveted for more modern high-rise hotels along the beach.

7

BUSINESS BOOM

One of the first businesses serving passengers riding the train to Myrtle Beach was the Burroughs & Collins commissary built in 1901. It was near the Pine Island train depot where the Chapin Company building was later located, near present-day Oak Street at Ninth Avenue North. The Myrtle Beach Post Office replaced the Withers Post Office, and it was in the back of the commissary.

The commissary was a town hub and general store where employees of Myrtle Beach Farms went for all types of supplies. It was where they had to get supplies, because the company paid them in tokens that were redeemable only at the commissary. The plain rectangular two-story building was longer than it was wide, with a one-story warehouse jutting off to the side.

A 1912 deal struck between Burroughs & Collins and New York investor Simeon Chapin "was the largest single land transfer in Horry County history," the company's own written history says. "They chose to name the company Myrtle Beach Farms because the land involved was primarily farmland used for growing Irish potatoes." Chapin put up money and Burroughs transferred fifty-three coastal land tracts from Burroughs & Collins to Myrtle Beach Farms Company. The new company's purpose was "developing Myrtle Beach into a major resort."

The company history quotes Henry B. Burroughs Jr. (1935–2009) regarding the deal:

The stock consisted of 2,000 shares at $100 par value. The initial offering by the board of incorporation was at $150 per share, $100 to capital stock and $50 to the surplus fund. The initial stock subscription consisted of Burroughs & Collins Company, 1,997 shares; F.A. Burroughs, one share; D.M. Burroughs, one share; and J.E. Bryan, one share. The capital stock subscribed was $200,000, and the capital surplus was $100,000. Burroughs & Collins Company's payment for its 1,997 shares consisted of 64,631 acres of land,…furniture and fixtures; growing crops; merchandise; artesian well and equipment; accounts receivable, cotton gin and equipment; saw mill; and cash; for a total of $299,550.

Around 1915, as tensions in Europe that led to World War I were heating up, a man named Captain Marshall Nance (1860–1944) had a sandwich stand near the Myrtle Beach railroad depot where he sold cornbread fish sandwiches for a nickel. By the early 1920s, Myrtle Beach had hot dog stands with ice cream and candy.

The war ended in late 1918, and the next year the Eighteenth Amendment was ratified to create a thirteen-year prohibition against the sale of alcoholic beverages. As a vacation destination, Myrtle Beach had its share of imbibers. Prohibition didn't slow those folks down much, and "in Horry County, the new law for the most part was simply ignored," Blanche Floyd wrote in a 2003 article published in *Sandlapper Magazine*. Locals had home brew sources for "wine, corn 'likker,' stump-hole whiskey or 'white lightning.'"

For people with more refined tastes, bottled spirits were smuggled into Murrells Inlet and Little River. Around 1930 or 1931, Floyd wrote, one such ship carrying "fine wine and whiskey" ran aground near Second Avenue Pier in Myrtle Beach. The crew abandoned ship, and "people converged on the grounded ship as if flares had been lit or rockets fired. Small groups approached quietly, eager to get their share of the contraband. Small boats ferried cases and bottles to shore, where the haul was divided. On the beach, others were waiting with small carts, wheelbarrows, children's wagons—anything that could carry a load." However, the end of Prohibition did not mean unfettered alcohol sales in Myrtle Beach. Bar business was brisk, but there have been blue laws and restrictions on alcohol sales far into the twenty-first century. By 2014, most have been repealed. Liquor by the drink is sold seven days a week in bars and restaurants, with the proper permitting, and beer and wine is available at all times at grocery and convenience stores. The sale of whole bottles of spirits like whiskey and vodka is permitted only in state-

Delta Drug Co. was within the Chapin Company department store, as shown in this 1936 photo by Bayard Wooten. *Horry County Museum, Conway, South Carolina.*

authorized Alcohol Beverage Control stores during proscribed operating hours, which do not include Sundays.

The Chapin Company department store replaced the Burroughs & Collins commissary in 1928, and it was in business through 1992. The store provided an extensive array of goods and services and was a major socialization spot. It also made deliveries. Since telephones didn't come to the beach until 1935, employees made rounds to inquire what supplies people needed, which would be delivered later. While it would be fair to call it a general store, it was much more, as described by Blanche Floyd in a 1993 article:

> *The building, about a third as large as it is now, had space for a drugstore, doctor's office, post office, S.C. Public Service Authority office, Myrtle Beach Farms Co. office, and the store…The store began with departments for groceries, clothing and piece goods, furniture and hardware. As the town grew, so did Chapin's, to 18 departments, some housed in separate buildings. Originally the store fronted on Broadway and Main streets, with houses close behind in what is now the parking lot. In 1958, a major expansion extended the building southward, and the parking lot was paved. Chapin's free delivery service was useful to everyone, especially senior citizens…An order called in before 9 a.m. was delivered by noon…Many people had charge accounts with the store. This simplified ordering by phone or sending your children to buy a gift. The clerks knew most of the customers and their children, so they would simply charge the purchase to the right "Mom" or "Dad." The store was a gathering place for friends to meet, shop, exchange*

The rear of the Chapin Company wasn't as glamorous as the front, but the parking lot supplemented limited street parking. *Horry County Museum, Conway, South Carolina.*

news or choice bits of gossip. With a beauty shop in the building, ladies could have their hair done, shop, eat a sandwich and fountain drink in the drugstore and spend a delightful day with friends.

Kathleen Futrell remembers often buying furniture at Chapin's:

Mattresses, box springs, chairs, rocking chairs, just about anything. And they had good credit. You'd just go right up there to that window and charge it. You could get a check cashed right there at that window, no problems. That was a tremendous store. After [walking by] the post office window, you'd go to the furniture [area] and then to the dry goods store and then to like a gift area, where you could buy all kinds of gifts and toys, [and then] to the grocery department and then their office up there where [store employees worked]. They had that whole block with the drugstore next to it, and Myrtle Beach Farms had their offices. Then there was a doctor's office and a barbershop. The Shell station was right across from Chapin Company on a little island out there. It was very small. It was one of the first gas stations in Myrtle Beach.

A 1955 advertisement for "Chapin Co." boasted it was "The Complete Store" with a grocery, market, seafood, dry goods, shoes, furniture, hardware, building supplies, fuel oil and the Chapin Service Station.

Kathleen Futrell also remembers Edward's Five-and-Ten that was downtown and sold everything from bobby pins and hair bows to warm peanuts and detergent. The Glamour Shop sold ladies' dresses, while Owen's Grocery Store had penny candy. Platt's Pharmacy was across the street from Delta Drug Store, and Johnson's Drug Store was also downtown. Cannon's Grocery Store was in the downtown building that became a hobby shop. Since Futrell had a business selling snow cones and ice cream, she "bought tons of ice" from the Crystal Ice Company. "Junior Bellamy used to haul that ice down the boulevard in three-hundred-pound blocks, and he would cut it into one-hundred-pound things and put it across his shoulders and bring it in."

The quickly growing Myrtle Beach area was a natural choice for business conventions, and that quickly grew into an important component of the local tourist economy. A coup was achieved in 1926 when the South Carolina Press Association had its annual meeting in Myrtle Beach, and in 1927, a group of bankers had their convention during the first week of June, which was the community's official season-opening week. The bankers came again in 1930, and that year, there was also a hardware convention, among many others.

Tourists and locals need to know what's going on around town, and on June 1, 1935, Kathleen Futrell's father, James Clarence Macklen, and his

Beginning in 1935, James Clarence Macklen (pictured) and his brother-in-law, C.L. Phillips, published the *Myrtle Beach News* out of a warehouse located behind Macklen's Sea Food. *Kathleen Futrell collection.*

Macklen's Sea Food featured seafood and hand-cut meats, but it also was a general grocery store. James Clarence Macklen is second from the right. *Kathleen Futrell collection.*

brother-in-law, C.L. Phillips, published the first edition of the *Myrtle Beach News* from a warehouse behind Macklen's Sea Food. A weekly at first, it became a daily on September 14, 1955.

"Chapin's had the first grocery store," Futrell said, "and my dad had the second…It was seafood in the back of it, but he had the canned goods, all groceries. It featured seafood and meats cut by a butcher." Macklen's Sea Food was located at the intersection of U.S. 501 and Broadway Street, and it had to be moved when 501 was built.

The next summer, on June 17, 1936, "Seacoast Telephone Co. installed 25 phones," according to a *Sun News* history item from November 16, 1999. "The directory occupied two paragraphs in the local newspaper." In 1937, the Colonial Coffee Shop was at the intersection of East Broadway Street and Kings Highway.

Streets in downtown Myrtle Beach at that time were wide and sandy with a few palmetto trees. The 2009 Horry County Historic Resources Survey says there were "a number of Spanish Revival buildings (such as Chapin Company), with stucco exteriors, wide arched entries, and faux projecting roofs clad in Spanish tile, while other structures were exposed brick…The Town developed along a small grid of squares, with the parallel streets following the angle of the coast."

The Colonial Coffee Shop, on the right, was at the intersection of East Broadway Street and Kings Highway. Beside it with columns is the H.B. Springs real estate office, which was moved off Oak Street. *Horry County Museum, Conway, South Carolina.*

From 1940 to 1950, the year-round population of Myrtle Beach doubled to 3,345 residents, and through the 1950s, the city continued to grow at a rapid pace. Large swaths of vegetation were lost to development such as amusement parks, campgrounds, motels, restaurants, golf courses and other tourist-geared businesses.

Much enhancement to the Myrtle Beach infrastructure took place in the 1950s, including the expansion of the Chapin Co. department store, and by the 1960s, the boom was on. The 2009 Horry County Historic Resources Survey describes the appearance of the changes:

> *The beach town was continuously* [sic] *adding new amenities, including the Pavilion Amusement Park, created by the Myrtle Beach Farms Company. Campgrounds sprung* [sic] *up along the major highway routes, sporting various fantasy themes to attract tourists. Motels welcomed the motorists and kept a similar theme of architecture, with stuccoed exteriors painted in bright colors and flat roofs, new and sometimes unusual building materials consisting of concrete screen walls and glass block, and attractive signage. Small suburbs grew up west of Myrtle Beach, towards the Intracoastal Waterway, and eventually crossed it, but the coastline filled in*

the fastest…Golf courses sprang up to accommodate the retiring "snowbirds" and northern golfers who enjoyed the snow-free courses in winter months, a significant physical change that marked Myrtle Beach as a year-round tourist destination rather than a small town.

INTEGRATING THE BEACH

The fight for African Americans' civil rights was turbulent during the 1940s, '50s and '60s, and previous racial segregation lines were blurred and challenged. The "deadline" or, sometimes "dead line," in Horry County that ran from Loris to Aynor in the early 1900s had relaxed over the years, and there were black communities throughout the area. Black residents and visitors were no longer threatened with being shot if they crossed the dead line, and there was a "black section" of Myrtle Beach, but segregation was the norm. However, during the post–World War II years, the South Carolina Ku Klux Klan resurged.

It didn't help racial tensions that a younger generation of white residents enjoyed going to a certain "black" Myrtle Beach nightclub to learn a slower version of the jitterbug that became known as shag dancing, or the "dirty shag." The beach had a more progressive racial attitude among the younger folks, and some of their parents didn't like it.

In 1950, Charlie Fitzgerald owned Charlie's Place at Whispering Pines, aka the Whispering Pine. It was a nightclub and restaurant where many of America's best black performers came to sing and play. The Whispering Pines section off Carver Street in Myrtle Beach is "on 'the Hill,' a black neighborhood only a stone's throw from the noisy, neon-lit oceanfront pavilion and amusement park that now dominates the tourist district in Myrtle Beach," wrote Frank Beacham in his 2003 essay titled "This Magic Moment: When the Ku Klux Klan Tried to Kill Rhythm & Blues Music in South Carolina." Fitzgerald also owned a motel, gas station, cab company and perhaps a brothel.

Fitzgerald certainly brought world-class acts to town. Myrtle Beach restaurateur Dino Thompson remembers seeing Little Richard perform there, and Beacham mentions Billie Holiday, Ray Charles, Count Basie, Duke Ellington and Lena Horne.

Fitzgerald was known as a sharp dresser, and he always carried a .45 and a .38 in over-the-shoulder holsters. "Dirty dancing" was an arrestable offense back then, and he allowed young whites to dance with blacks at Charlie's

Place. Neither Klan members nor a majority of the white-dominated Myrtle Beach population liked Fitzgerald, but a significant number of young whites almost idolized his club's music and the sexy dangerousness he emanated.

The Klan was stirred to antagonism in the summer of 1950 by a fiery election campaign for a South Carolina U.S. Senate seat when many racial segregationist threats were made. Throughout Horry County, the Klan staged nighttime parades, complete with hoods and burning crosses. One such parade was organized to start at 9:00 p.m. on Saturday, August 26, 1950, to run in front of Charlie's Place. It wasn't unexpected because Fitzgerald, according to Beacham's essay, had been warned by Klan members to not allow any more whites into his club.

An article dated August 30, 1950, in the *Tabor City Tribune* (Tabor City, North Carolina, is about a forty-five-minute drive northwest of Myrtle Beach) included information about what may have contributed to the animosity against Fitzgerald. "Persons in that area say that Fitzgerald's businesses included the operation of a taxi fleet, the operation of a dance hall, where the violence occurred, and the operation of several tourist cabins. The cabin phase of his operations was generally believed to be some what [*sic*] of a shady nature. However, no official reports have been forthcoming in this regard."

As for the parade of twenty-seven cars and its resulting violence, the same article says:

> *"Details of a Ku Klux Klan–Negro gun fight in Myrtle Beach Saturday night during which a Conway policeman, wearing a klan robe over his uniform was shot to death, remained sketchy tonight," the Associated Press said Tuesday in an article date-lined in Conway…Killed during the gun fight, which took place in the colored section of Myrtle Beach about midnight, was James Daniel Johnson, 42, who was shot under the left shoulder blade with what is believed to be a .38 caliber pistol. Johnson was carried to the Conway Hospital but died a few minutes after being admitted. It has been impossible to find the names of the persons carrying Johnson to the hospital. Horry County Sheriff C. Ernest Sasser, according to the Associated Press report, said that "300 shots were fired by about 60 robed klansmen and an unknown number of negroes in front of a dance hall and tourist court." Johnson was wearing both his police uniform and a klansman's robe at the time he was shot.*

During the attack, Charlie's Place was shot up and wrecked, inside and out. Charlie Fitzgerald was beaten and had his ear cut. He was held in protective police custody in Columbia, and no charges were filed against him in relation to the violence that day. Other African Americans injured that night were thirty-year-old Gene Nichols, who was shot in the foot; Charlie Vance, "about 30," who had internal injuries; and Cynthia "Shag" Harrol, who was "hit in the back several times and required medical attention."

In addition to the death of Conway police officer/Klansman James Johnson, there were several Klansmen arrests related to the Charlie's Place incident: South Carolina grand dragon Thomas Hamilton, Conway optician Dr. A.J. Gore, Conway native and Klan secretary-treasurer J.C. Creel, Florence beer truck driver R.L. Sims, Horry County farmer June Cartrette, Bill Bennett, Boyd Ford, Roy Ford, Edwin B. Floyd and Rarien Britt. They were charged with inciting mob violence, but some weren't prosecuted for lack of evidence. The rest had their cases go before a grand jury, which declined to prosecute.

Charlie Fitzgerald continued to operate his club, but it was never the same as before the Ku Klux Klan attack. Fitzgerald died of natural causes in 1955. The heyday of black soul music was lost forever, and the birthplace of shag dancing in Myrtle Beach was gone.

The 2009 Horry County Historic Resources Survey notes the neighborhood where Charlie's Place was located has only remnants of its history. It says:

> There are at least two historically African-American communities within Myrtle Beach, the Canal Street neighborhood and Booker T. Washington area. Both contain remnants of a self-contained community with homes, churches, commercial and entertainment sites, and even motels, examples of a self-reliant district created by segregation, and popular during the 1940s through 1960s. Integration has left these communities with smaller populations and less demands for commercial buildings, which has left some of them vacant or altered for different uses.

POST-STORM SURGE

The year 1955 marked a concerted effort to promote Myrtle Beach as a year-round destination. The chamber of commerce wanted to let the world know that Hurricane Hazel didn't destroy the town, and many press releases and promotional materials sent that message. A twenty-page marketing

Sun-fun

AROUND MYRTLE BEACH

A COMPLIMENTARY COPY
from
The Publisher

Myrtle Beach Pavilion

August 14, 1955

FREE
To Tourists

In 1955, publications such as this were widely distributed to let tourists know Hurricane Hazel didn't blow the town away. *Author's collection.*

pamphlet called *Sun-fun Around Myrtle Beach* published on August 14, 1955, highlights many of the businesses of the day.

Boat races were held on Myrtle Beach Lakes at the Pine Island Bridge off U.S. 501, two miles west of town. Every Saturday night, car races were held at the Myrtle Beach Race Track, and there was dancing at the Ocean Forest Hotel, the Myrtle Beach Pavilion, Haley's Party Restaurant (at First Avenue South and Kings Highway) and the Ocean Terrace Restaurant at the "south end of Myrtle Beach on the Ocean Front." Several piers offered fishing, and there were three golf courses (the Dunes Golf Club, Pine Lakes Country Club and Conway Golf Club), two driving ranges and three miniature golf courses.

In 1955, amusement rides could be found at the pavilion and the Gay Dolphin Park on Ocean Boulevard, Jungle Land (a sort of zoo) was off Kings Highway, Fish Hook Skating Rink was at Pine Island Bridge and public tennis courts were located behind Myrtle Beach High School and next to the Ocean Forest Hotel.

8

WASHINGTON PARK RACE TRACK

In 2014, the Washington Park Horse Race Track site is an empty lot full of asphalt and small flowering trees, but from June 3, 1938, through 1947, brothers from Mullins named Paul and Parrot Hardy invested $40,000 to build the racetrack. It was located just north of the intersection of Oak Street and Twenty-first Avenue North on land leased from Myrtle Beach Farms. The clay racetrack featured a steel grandstand with room for 5,200 spectators to watch harness racing and gaze at the nearby ocean. In harness racing, the horses, called trotters and pacers, pull a rig and driver.

"This elaborate racing complex included a half-mile track, stables for 150 horses, and semi-weekly races with an average $250 purse," the Myrtle Beach Comprehensive Plan says. "Washington Park Race Track was built with the hopes that the South Carolina Legislature would abolish the anti-gambling laws."

"Race Track at Myrtle Beach to Open Today" was the lead sports story in the June 3, 1938 edition of the *Florence Morning News*. Grand festivities were scheduled with a celebratory steering committee composed of Myrtle Beach mayor W.L. Harrelson, chamber of commerce president J.N. Ramsey, *Myrtle Beach News* editor J.P. Winningham, Lions Club secretary Frank Hughes, attorney and American Legion commander Joseph W. Little and chamber of commerce public relations director Colonel H.B. Springs. South Carolina governor Olin D. Johnston came for the festivities along with Charleston mayor Burnet R. Maybank and about five thousand spectators. As for the racing:

The Washington Park Race Track featured harness racing, and city leaders passed a special ordinance allowing gambling as an amusement, which bypassed state anti-gambling laws. *Author's collection.*

Approximately sixty of the nation's fastest trotting and pacing horses are now stabled at Washington Park and more are arriving daily. During the course of the week it was revealed that Wilt Reynolds, tobacco magnate of Winston-Salem, whose stable of over 100 thoroughbreds is an institution among the followers of turf and track, will enter eight of his favorites in the Myrtle Beach competition. The Reynolds horses will be stabled at Washington Park for the summer…For two and one half hours the spectators will witness three thrilling races of three heats each as horses and drivers compete for the coveted prize of $250 for the winner of each race.

A June 1938 advertisement says three harness races with nine or more heats and "trotting and pacing" would be run on Wednesday, June 29. Several new horses were running, and "a hefty purse" was ready for the winners. Purses that year on July 2 and July 4 ranged from $300 to $500. A July 1938 advertisement in the Lumberton, North Carolina *Robesonian* says the park was "where the Turf Meets the Surf!"

When its season opened on Memorial Day (May 30) in 1939, it was "the scene of a trotting matinee on Tuesday and the following day races will be included on the schedule. These races will continue every Wednesday and Saturday through June and July, also into August."

In April 1940, the racetrack made news in the Harness Racing Notes of the *Dunkirk Evening Observer* in New York. "It is pleasant to report that Paul Hardy, Mullins and Myrtle Beach, S.C., [are] going to put the trotters over again at Washington Park, Myrtle Beach this summer. It was reported this spring that the bang-tails would hold sway. As a part of the Civitan convention there May 18, a race program will be staged, reports C.A. Hopkins, and the season will really open Decoration Day." Bangtails are racehorses that have their tails cut straight across so they resemble tassels, and the writer was referring to racehorses that carry riders on their backs rather than pulling a horse and rig. Decoration Day is the former name of Memorial Day.

A large advertisement—almost a quarter page—on the sports page of the June 5, 1940 issue of the *Florence Morning News* says "Races!" in capitalized bold letters about three inches high. "Every Wednesday and Saturday at the Washington Park Race Track, Myrtle Beach, S.C. 100 of the Finest Horses in the South! Our Races This Year Are More Exciting and Better Than Ever Before. Of Special Interest to Those Having Half Holidays Every Wednesday. Our Post Time Is 3 P.M."

Washington Park Race Track operated for nine years, and eventually, dog racing was added to the lineup. But in 1947, all hope was removed that parimutuel betting would be legalized in South Carolina. Other forms of betting described as "amusement" were tried with the passage of a special ordinance by Myrtle Beach city leaders, but the South Carolina legislature didn't approve of any gambling, no matter what it was called. An impetus to

Races were held every Wednesday and Saturday at the Washington Park Race Track. *Horry County Museum, Conway, South Carolina.*

banish gambling included several church leaders from around the state who spoke out against it and attended legal proceedings to protest the practice.

A small item in the July 3, 1947 edition of the Statesville, North Carolina *Landmark* newspaper says:

> *Officials of the Washington Park race track are making plans for a crowd of seven thousand fans for a six-race program that's to be run on tomorrow's holiday card. The promoters are protected by an injunction that keeps sheriffs and constabulary officers from raiding. At the Myrtle Beach track they don't call it betting. They have so-called "contribution" windows where the patrons can "contribute." Early this week, Governor Strom Thurmond said he planned a visit to Myrtle Beach but he wouldn't attend the races if there was any betting.*

On July 16, 1947, an article in the *Florence Morning News* said track operator M.O. Parson was in court in Kingstree over gambling charges that, if enforced, would result in a $1,000 fine for each race.

Senator P.H. McEachin of Florence argued in favor of betting on races, claiming that "the practice of 'mutual guessing' was only a 'legalized method' of giving away cash prizes to contributors at the races" and emphasized that "the municipality of Myrtle Beach from whom a license to operate a race track there had been obtained, had passed an ordinance legalizing the 'amusement' form of horse racing." On that day, Judge J. Frank Eatmon allowed one more week of operation at Washington Park Race Track.

It may have been a coincidence, but on July 25, 1947, members of the South Carolina Sheriff's Association had a convention in Myrtle Beach.

On August 9, 1947, the *Florence Morning News* reported that Judge Eatmon did not vacate his order that prevented law enforcement officers from shutting down the racetrack for violating South Carolina gambling laws. It says, "A survey of press releases, including that on the judge's opinion, indicates that adoption of the terms 'guessing' for 'betting' and substitution of 'contributions' for placing money on bets is nothing more or less than an effort to circumvent the law in South Carolina against trace track gambling." On August 15, the case went to the South Carolina Supreme Court when the state sought to overrule circuit judge Eatmon's refusal to vacate the injunction to shut down betting in Myrtle Beach.

On August 16, an article headlined "Race Tracks Close" ran in the *Florence Morning News*:

The race tracks here called it quits today (August 15) after a state Supreme Court justice cleared the way for officers to clamp down on a novel betting system known as "equal mutual guessing." Only a few more hours after associate Justice C. Dewey Oxner had stayed a lower court injunction against the state, M.O. Parsons, one of the operators of the tracks here, announced the closing of the tracks. He said horses and dogs which have run in the races would be shipped to other points immediately.

Hope that gambling on horse and dog races lingered. A November 1948 article in the *Aiken Standard and Review* says:

The "horse race bill" may bob up again in the 1949 General Assembly, according to recent reports. The bill, which would legalize betting on horse races in counties voting for it in popular elections, almost became law in 1947. It got off to a fast start, cleared the House of Representatives easily, but faded in the home stretch in the Senate. The bill never came to a showdown vote, but died when the legislature adjourned in 1948. An unofficial poll taken by supporters indicated the bill would have passed if all Senators voted on the question. Proponents of the measure, reports say, may bring up the bill in 1949 as a "revenue producing measure." They probably will argue that the state needs the money that would be derived from taxes on wagers.

In 1951, Edward Canne reopened the racetrack and named it the Myrtle Beach Raceway. A 2014 article in *Hoof Beats*, the magazine of the U.S. Trotting Association, says Canne "intended on making it a winter training haven for Standardbreds, but without legalized gambling it was unable to generate enough revenue to stay afloat." It closed in 1952, and Barbara Stokes says in *Greetings from…Myrtle Beach: A History, 1900–1980* that part of the site was used in 1953 as a golf driving range, complete with night lights. From 1955 through '57, it was opened as Coastal Speedway and NASCAR races were held there until Myrtle Beach Speedway (called the RAMBI Race Track at that time, which stood for the Racing Association of Myrtle Beach Inc.) opened a few miles west of Myrtle Beach off U.S. 501. Washington Park Race Track's steel grandstand was moved to that location.

In 1958, the original track site served a useful purpose when "a light plane piloted by Dr. John Flaherty of Southern Pines, N.C., made an emergency landing" there. The pilot was unhurt, and "his craft was slightly damaged." In the 1970s, Myrtle Square Mall was built at the racetrack site, and it was

In this 1953 photo of the Myrtle Beach coastline, the racetrack can be seen at the upper right. *Author's collection.*

a vibrant business until it was demolished in 2006. Although the land is idle in 2014 except for special events like car shows and a traveling circus, a faint impression of an oval track can still be seen.

9

SHOW TIME

T heater shows were performed at the pavilion and at the Myrtle Beach Playhouse at the Ocean Forest Hotel. Movies were shown at Ben's Broadway Theater on Main Street, which was the first Myrtle Beach movie theater; it opened in 1936. A few more of the city's many movie theaters were the Gloria Theater (circa 1937) on Ninth Avenue North, the Flamingo Drive-In at Seventy-seventh Avenue North and the Myrtle Drive-In.

Johnny Butler of Myrtle Beach remembers going to the Broadway Theater in the 1950s and '60s. "Saturday was a double feature, and it was fourteen cent to get into the movie," he said. "Popcorn was a nickel or dime, soda about the same...There was a two-cent deposit on the bottle. Good days."

The Rivoli Theatre, which opened in 1958 on Chester Street in Myrtle Beach, was "designed by architect Harold J. Riddle," according to scmovietheatres.com, and its exterior was noted for having

> *two abstract (nude) figures, male and female, holding up the columns of the theatre façade,* [that were] *commissioned by Mr. Riddle and created by artist Gerard Tempest* [who]...*attained an international reputation in the art world. The figures are made of reinforced cement, and many coats of paint have covered them since their creation. Inside the Rivoli there also remains a bas-relief mural, artist unknown.*

The theater had 1,078 seats, including a balcony; a lobby with terrazzo floors and walnut paneling; and an innovative (for that period) four-

Plane Schedule:

Flight 55.
Arrive from Wilmington, N. C., 9:00 a.m..
Leave for Charlotte, Asheville, Cincinnati: 9:03 a.m.
Flight 27.
Arrive from Wilmington, N. C., 3:45 p.m.
Leave for Charlotte, Asheville, Cincinnati: 3:48 p.m.
Flight 50.
Arrive from Cincinnati, Asheville, Charlotte: 1:31 p.m.
Leave for Wilmington, N. C.: 1:34 p.m.
Flight 52.
Arrive from Cincinnati, Asheville, Charlotte: 5:03 p.m.
Leave for Wilmington, N. C.: 5:06 p.m.
Flight 6.
Arrive from Louisville, Charlotte: 10:02 p.m.
Leave for Wilmington, N. C.: 10:05 p.m.

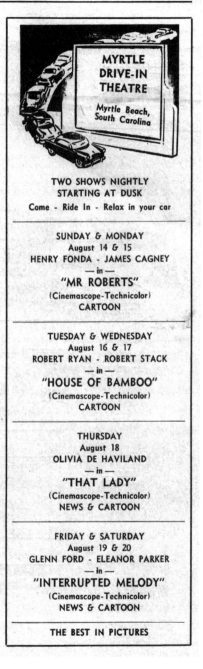

Myrtle Beach had many drive-in theaters, like the Myrtle Drive-In in this 1953 advertisement. *Author's collection.*

When *Don't Make Waves* starring Tony Curtis was filmed, the skydiving sequence was remarkable for the times because it was done with a helmet camera. *Author's collection.*

channel stereophonic sound system. The first movie shown there on June 19, 1958, was *This Happy Feeling*, starring Debbie Reynolds.

In 1967, during the Sun Fun Festival, the world premiere of *Don't Make Waves*, starring Tony Curtis, was held at the Rivoli. That film also starred Sharon Tate, who was murdered two years later in California by the Charles Manson followers while she was pregnant and married to filmmaker Roman Polanski. Making cameo appearances were Jim Backus (Thurston Howell III in "Gilligan's Island") and ventriloquist Edgar Bergen. The movie's skydiving sequence took thirty-five takes with a helmet camera and resulted in the death of one of the stuntmen who landed in the Pacific Ocean and drowned.

Many Myrtle Beach natives remember going to the Rivoli on Saturday mornings and paying their admission with bottle caps. Karon Bowers Jones did in the 1960s:

> *I remember when I was little, every Saturday morning we could get in with seven bottle caps—Coca-Cola bottle caps. You bring in seven, and you got to go in. And we saw, I believe, two movies. They were not extremely long; they had to be kids' movies because it was all for kids…Patsy Walker who is Patsy Lott now [and] who lives in Goose Creek, South Carolina—we used to go together, every Saturday, and I can see the candy that we got.*

They're caramel on the outside and a white creamy thing in the middle, kind of like a Charleston Chew…and then both of us got, they were called Lucky Charms suckers…They were a big, flat sucker, and it was about the size of a half dollar…But that's a fond memory, the Rivoli Theatre. And around the corner was the Gloria Theater, which we didn't think was as glorious.

The Rivoli, which operated until the 1980s, is, according to the 2009 historic property survey, Myrtle Beach's "only surviving mid-century movie theater":

Constructed in 1950, it is the finest example of its type in the county, but it faces the threat of neglect and is very near the recently demolished Pavilion amusement park. Pressure emanating from the new development at that site may impact the theater negatively. Of greater concern is that although the City of Myrtle Beach pledged funds to develop the site as a performing and visual arts center, within the past few months, they have entertained proposals for a larger cultural arts complex at a different site. The City purchased the 1,000-seat theater around 1999 [for $700,000].

A nonprofit group was launched in 2004 to raise funds to remodel and operate the theater again as a "venue for non-profit art organizations," but in 2011, the City of Myrtle Beach started leasing the Rivoli Theatre to a nonprofit teen ministry called Ground Zero. A 2008 article about the Rivoli written by Kimberly Moore and published in *Weekly Surge* said the two Riddle sculptures outside the theater "have been removed to the Myrtle Beach Convention Center for safekeeping" and that their value had "increased to more than $250,000." In 2013, Myrtle Beach voters approved funding for a new 850-seat performing arts center to be constructed beside the Myrtle Beach Convention Center, and Moore's article said the Riddle sculptures would be placed there "to continue the atmosphere of the old Rivoli." However, in the spring of 2014, construction had not started on a new performing arts center.

AMUSEMENTS

While the Myrtle Beach Pavilion was the most well-known family fun spot in Myrtle Beach, many others have operated over the years.

Fort Caroline featured "life of an early Huguenot Village such as Charles Towne." *Jack Bourne collection.*

Fort Caroline was off U.S. 501 at Forestbrook Road in the 1960s. When it opened, it re-created the "life of an early Huguenot Village such as Charles Towne," a 1966 newspaper article says, and "there is even the capture, struggle, and conviction of a woman accused of being a witch." Following a trial, she was burned at the stake. Visitors saw hearth cooking, blacksmithing, candle making and other vintage occupations. Villagers did battle with Indians (college students from Lumberton, North Carolina) and Spanish explorers, and a bus resembling a covered wagon picked up visitors from Myrtle Beach. Celebrities made guest appearances, and Ed Herian of Murrells Inlet remembers seeing Dan Blocker (1928–1972), who played Hoss Cartwright on *Bonanza*.

In its last couple years, many locals say that "hippies took it over," but it actually became a venue for rock concerts.

Jungle Land was off Kings Highway around Ninth Avenue South and operated for many years starting in the 1940s. "It had pink flamingos, monkeys, all kinds of exotic animals," Jack Bourne said. It also had parrots that posed on people's shoulders, alligators, deer and "bear cubs begging for peanuts" a postcard says.

Serpent City was at the north end of Myrtle Beach off Restaurant Row, where Chuck's Steak House is now at 9695 North Kings Highway. It had more than snakes, Mike McKinnon remembers. He and his brother, Kevin, were about nine or ten years old when their father worked at his restaurant next door to Serpent City. "I remember there was an old lion, a really old lion. His name was Gus. He didn't have any teeth, [he was] declawed, just totally harmless…They had alligators, they had monkeys."

Serpent City also had deer, and in 1968, its owners, Lee "Slim" Rowan and King Martin, were angry, according to a newspaper report, when someone breached the fence, shot a European fallow deer, took its horns and body and left the hornless head behind for a dog to drag home. The buck, named Daddy Deer, was tame and let children pet it.

In 1966, Grand Strand Amusement Park opened near Withers Swash at Third Avenue South. It had a renowned wooden roller coaster called the Swamp Fox.

In 1973, seven people were injured during Easter weekend when a chairlift partially collapsed. "The accident occurred about 9:30 p.m. in the Grand Strand Amusement Park in Myrtle Beach," an article in the *Burlington Daily Times News* of Burlington, North Carolina, said, "when a T-shaped arm supporting the chair lift's cables snapped. Police said the cables sagged, causing at least two chair lifts to dump their occupants." New owners changed its name in 1992 to Family Kingdom Amusement Park, and it was operating seasonally as of the spring of 2014. The Swamp Fox roller coaster is still there and is the only wooden roller coaster in South Carolina.

The Astro Needle was, as the name suggests, a tall and thin two-hundred-foot-high structure with an elevator. It was located across from the Myrtle Beach Pavilion. Mike McKinnon of Myrtle Beach said the elevator slowly spiraled up to the top. He also remembers it had a spiral sidewalk leading to it where he enjoyed skateboarding. It was taken down in the 1980s.

Gay Dolphin Park operated for almost the entire decade of the 1960s, and it was located a short distance down the beach from the Myrtle Beach Pavilion. It was known for the Wild Mouse—a roller coaster that looked like a giant boxy Tinker Toy—and its oceanfront arcade.

PirateLand amusement park, which opened in 1964, was just south of Myrtle Beach on Kings Highway where Lakewood Camping Resort and Pirateland Campground are today. As the name says, it had a pirate theme with actors playing the roles of swashbucklers and having sword fights in the streets. Karon Bowers Jones remembers dancing in a show there at age fifteen in "the last little theater on the right-hand side."

A section of PirateLand had stagecoach rides. Ed Herian of Murrells Inlet worked for the local ambulance squad at the time, and he responded to a call in June 1966 when a stagecoach overturned: "A coach was coming in and going around the bend, and the back wheel just broke. As that coach

Right: The Astro Needle had an elevator that rotated and allowed for a panoramic view of Myrtle Beach. *Author's collection.*

Below: The Gay Dolphin gift shop had an oceanfront amusement park during the 1960s. The Myrtle Beach Pavilion is on the left. *Author's collection.*

turned over, a little kid was being thrown out, and the coach came down and hit him. He died."

PirateLand closed in 1972, and it reopened in 1975, when Summerset Group of Charlotte, North Carolina, operated it. The same year, it defaulted on a $1.9 million loan, according to the *Statesville Record & Landmark*. Later in 1975, North Carolina National Bank sold the mortgage to Harry Koch, an experienced amusement park owner, for $1.9 million. In 1976, Harry Koch, and his stepson, Carl Derk, were murdered in a shooting that took place in a mobile home at the park, where they lived. In 1977, NCNB was the only bidder on the park and got the remainder of the thirty-year lease for $620,000, which was then purchased by the Perry family of Lakewood Camping Resort.

Also in 1977, a seven-hundred-pound dolphin that locals named Patrick beached itself in Surfside Beach. Attempts to put it back in the ocean failed, and a newspaper article says, "He was captured and placed in an aquatic dome pool at Lakewood Magic Harbor" where he "seemed reasonably happy in the pool, frolicking with Jenny and Pepper, a pair of mature dolphins who were about half his size." However, Patrick soon died.

The Perrys had Magic Harbor for several years and added the Magic Mountain water slide, a log flume, an antique car ride, the Corkscrew roller coaster that turned riders upside down, a lighthouse and more. They also introduced a music variety show called High Steppin' Country that is still performed during the summer season at Lakewood Camping Resort. A 1977 article in the *Charleston News and Courier* said a hot air balloon was added to the park's eighteen rides, and an entrance fee was no longer charged.

Magic Harbor was at the site of the former PirateLand, a little south of Myrtle Beach State Park off Kings Highway. *Author's collection.*

Ride tickets cost thirty to seventy-five cents. The park had a "creekfront boardwalk" and "sidewalk restaurants and shops that line the main street of the park."

In 1982, the park was leased to an English firm called Blackpool Leisure Park Company, and the entertainment took on British flair. However, in April 1983, a young teenager died from injuries received while on a roller coaster called the Black Witch, also known as the Galaxy. Magic Harbor closed for good later that year, and eventually, it was razed to become part of two adjacent campgrounds. Locals often refer to the park as Tragic Harbor.

FANTASY HARBOUR

In 1977, George Bishop opened a new home furnishings store called Waccamaw Pottery. Located just west of the Intracoastal Waterway, it became an extremely popular shopping venue for locals and busloads of tourists. The Pottery expanded through the years until it was a mall called Waccamaw Factory Shoppes with multiple buildings, about one hundred stores and a tram that shuttled people around its eighty acres. A 1986 article in the *Wilmington Star-News* said, "Last year five million persons, nearly twice the population of South Carolina, came looking for bargains in a discount shopping mall that was once a dusty, cement-floored pottery barn."

In 1999, the Waccamaw Corp., which owned the pottery, merged with HomePlace Stores Inc., and the name changed to Waccamaw Pottery & Linen. The store closed in 2001. The mall has deteriorated over the years despite efforts to revitalize it. One building contains a few shops, but most of it is deserted as of the spring of 2014.

It was logical for other business people to see the potential in offering entertainment to all those millions of shoppers. Starting in the early 1990s, theaters were built behind Waccamaw Pottery in an area dubbed Fantasy Harbour. First, there was Magic on Ice, a skating theater with one thousand seats. The Gatlin brothers' two-thousand-seat theater came next and was soon joined by the Cercle Theatre, the Ronnie Milsap Theatre and Medieval Times, a dinner theater where spectators watch twelfth-century entertainment like jousting and falconry.

The Gatlin brothers had their theater from 1994 to 1998, and then in 1999, it became the Crook and Chase Theater, where Charlie Chase and Lorianne Crook hosted their *Crook & Chase* television variety show that aired on the Nashville Network. A musical called *Summer of '66* was performed there at night. The television show was canceled, and in 2000, Crook and her husband, Jim Owens, announced they bought the building and were going to broadcast live television shows from there. One year later, the mortgage holder initiated foreclosure proceedings. Several acts and shows subsequently performed there, but none lasted long. As of the spring of 2014, the building is a church.

The Ronnie Milsap Theatre was open for two seasons in the mid-1990s and hosted a monthlong show by Fabian in 1996. It became the All American Theater, and then when a church purchased it, the theater was called the Forum. It's still a church in the spring of 2014.

The Savoy Theatre at Fantasy Harbour launched in 1995 with an ice skating variety show called Magic on Ice that later became Snoopy's Magic on Ice. The Savoy had a big band show in 1998, a Patsy Cline tribute show in 1999 and other shows. In 2000, a company called Renaissance Entertainment, whose president was Jon Binkowski, bought the theater, renamed it the Ice Castle and brought in Olympic skater Nancy Kerrigan

The former Savoy Theatre became the Ice Castle, and then it was absorbed into Hard Rock Park and became the Ice House Theater. *Photo by Jeremy Thompson.*

to star in a few shows. Binkowski went on to open Hard Rock Park and absorbed the theater into the park's property. As of the spring of 2014, the theater is unused.

Binkowski also owned the Cercle Theater, which looked like a circus tent and had previously been the show home of Euro Circus. Before it was dismantled to make room for Hard Rock Park, it had an ice skating rink the public could use.

As of the spring of 2014, Medieval Times is the only Fantasy Harbour theater still operating.

HARD LUCK PARK

In 2003, Binkowski let it be known he planned to build a theme park at Fantasy Harbour, and in 2006, he and Steven Goodwin, the chief operating officer of HRP Management Corp., announced they secured $400 million to start building the world's first Hard Rock Park on 55 acres (within a 140-acre

Hard Rock Park opened its gates on April 15, 2008. *Photo by Jeremy Thompson.*

site) around a small lake. Myrtle Beach locals were mixed in their reactions. Some were thrilled about such a unique attraction coming to the area, while others were skeptical that 55 acres could contain a viable amusement park. A groundbreaking ceremony in July 2006 featured a three-story sand sculpture called *Mount Rockmore* with the faces of Jimi Hendrix, Bob Marley, Elvis Presley and John Lennon. Hundreds of employees were hired before the park opened, and they enjoyed management's relaxed attitude that encouraged a rock star appearance.

Despite the skepticism, tickets to the park's grand opening on April 15, 2008, were coveted. Grand opening ticket prices were $272 and included concerts by the Eagles and the Moody Blues. Many locals who had business relationships with the park received free admission.

The park had six major areas flowing into one another around the lake, and the lake had a seventy-foot Gibson Les Paul guitar replica in the middle of it from which fireworks were shot every night at closing time the first couple months the park operated. At the entrance was the All Access Plaza with gift shops and the Whammy Bar, where local bands performed.

Heading to the left, the first area was Rock & Roll Heaven with a live show called Malibu Beach Party that included a lot of skilled diving into a swimming pool and ended with a smoked-out Volkswagen Bus. Nearby was Reggae River Falls, an enormous multilevel water play area with a giant bucket that dumped out a waterfall when it was full. The centerpiece of this area, and of the entire park, was the Led Zeppelin: The Ride roller coaster. Riders listened to Led Zeppelin's "Whole Lotta Love" before the ride started, and the song continued as the cars sped at sixty-five miles per hour through the fifteen-story-tall coaster with intense drops, loops and turns.

British Invasion had its own roller coaster called Maximum RPM! The setting was a manufacturing plant, and riders were in English convertible sports cars that were hoisted up a track to the top and let go for a steep and thrilling drop. However, the ride was frequently out of service. The British area also had a spinning ride with London taxis, an interactive phone booth, a double-decker bus, a merry-go-round with horses that looked medieval and a stunt show.

"I know a lot of people came to Hard Rock Park solely for the ball pit attraction in the British Invasion part of the park," Adam Billingsley said. He was a teenager while working at the park as a ride operator, and he had the same job the next year when it became Freestyle Music Park. "It was a three-story jungle gym with air pressured guns you loaded balls into and shot [at] people as they passed by, and a large container on the ceiling in the center of the room would unload plastic balls to everyone when it met its ball quota. That place was packed with kids every hour of the day."

Lost in the '70s had a dark ride that was the favorite of many visitors. Called Nights in White Satin: The Trip, riders heard music by the Moody Blues and experienced a psychedelic light show. An arcade area had vintage pinball and video game machines.

Born in the USA had an amphitheater called Hard Rock Live where well-known singers, such as KC and the Sunshine Band, performed, but not as many concerts were scheduled as season ticket holders were led to believe. This area also had a child's roller coaster and another adult coaster called Slippery When Wet, plus a couple children's play areas and a midway.

The final area was Cool Country, and that's where Binkowski used the former Ice Castle Theater, which was renamed the Ice House Theater and had a country rock show on ice. A hidden operator controlled a statue in front of the theater, and it interacted verbally with people and could spit water at them. Cool Country also had a roller coaster that was like riding in a mining car through an abandoned shaft.

Hard Rock Park had forty rides, which seemed skimpy to many visitors. "A main complaint everyone had was that Hard Rock Park didn't have enough rides," Billingsley said.

Each park section had at least one dining area that matched the theme. Lost in the '70s had a fine dining venue called Alice's Restaurant, and Arlo Guthrie visited for its opening.

Many people thought the one-day ticket price was too expensive at $50 for anyone older than age three. VIP passes that allowed going to the head of the line on rides and preferred seating for shows were $200, while an annual pass was $150. The VIP passes weren't a good deal, because lines were minimal. Binkowski and Goodwin were counting on attendance of twenty to thirty thousand per day, but those crowds didn't show up. Usually there were two to three thousand per day.

Nevertheless, many locals bought the season passes and thoroughly enjoyed frequent visits. "We lived [nearby] at the time," Michelle Johnson Householder said. "I'd get off work at 9:00 p.m., and the fireworks were at 10:00. We'd go in to have a beer and watch the fireworks. It was fun; I enjoyed it. They had the best fireworks I've ever seen outside Disney World."

The fireworks synced to "Another One Bites the Dust" by Queen, and on the Fourth of July, an especially extravagant fireworks show synced to "We Are the Champions." But with revenue nowhere near what was needed to pay the bills, Hard Rock Park started closing at 10:00 p.m.

Fireworks were shot from around Hard Rock Park's iconic giant guitar. *Photo by Jeremy Thompson.*

instead of 1:00 a.m., and daily fireworks changed to weekly fireworks on Saturdays.

The 2008 season ended a month earlier than anticipated. Most employees were laid off, and its owners filed for Chapter 11 bankruptcy protection. The decision was made to sell the park, which the bankruptcy court approved, and in February 2009, FPI MB Entertainment bought the $400 million park for $25 million. The Hard Rock theme could not be retained, and all the park's logo items had to be destroyed.

In May 2009, the newly named Freestyle Music Park opened. Many of the previous year's seasonal employees were rehired, but this time around, they had to maintain clean-cut appearances. Most of the rides and attractions were the same, but they all had new names and themes and in some cases were sad shadows of the Hard Rock Park glitz. Ticket prices went down to forty dollars for adults and thirty dollars for children, and annual passes were seventy-five dollars and forty-five dollars.

Despite getting an amusement park for a bargain price, Freestyle Music Park also lasted for only one season. Its demise has been a long tangle of

When Hard Rock Park closed after one season, many people saw the irony in the words on this gate from the Doors' lyrics which said, "When the music's over, turn out the light." *Photo by Jeremy Thompson.*

legal proceedings. On February 26, 2014, creditors received letters from the United States Bankruptcy Court in the District of Delaware informing them that HRP Myrtle Beach Management, LLC; We Got Your Back Security Co., LLC; HRP Myrtle Beach Holdings Capital Corp.; and HRP Capital Corp., all listed as debtors, changed their status from "asset to no asset." The letters say, "Having discovered no assets hereby gives Notice that this is a No Asset case."

People speculate about why neither park survived with theories ranging from the great recession to poor marketing to outright mismanagement. Some of the park's land has been sold as well as some rides, but in the spring of 2014, the bulk of the park sits deteriorating with weeds growing in its parking lots. In a town accustomed to rapid business turnovers, Hard Rock Park is the epitome of a one-season wonder.

Rapid Growth

City growth picked up in the 1970s, and tourism brought in more money than farming. In 1973, laws were changed so that alcohol could be served in bars and restaurants (no more brown bagging your own bottle), which helped spur an unprecedented amount of construction. A September 1973 article in the *Florence Morning News* says, "During the first six months of 1973, the city of Myrtle Beach issued more than 250 building permits which represented approximately $33 million in new structures. From the N.C. border to Pawley's [*sic*] Island there is hardly one mile of the resort area where a construction project cannot be seen." Projects noted in the article include "a $9 million shopping center" that would become Myrtle Square Mall; a $5.5 million seventeen-story condominium project, "which will cover the entire block between 17th and 18th avenues"; and another $4.8 million fourteen-story one-hundred-unit group of condos "between 6th and 7th Avenues." Also in 1973, Myrtle Beach was approved for a $630,000 grant from the U.S. Economic Development Administration to "help enlarge the local water system and stimulate long-range economic growth."

The article says in the works were "more than a dozen new motels, five restaurants, several regular and miniature golf courses, a heliport, 75 townhouse units and 291 condominium units."

In 1975, the town's first mall, Myrtle Square Mall, was opened at the site of the old Washington Park Race Track. It was during the '70s that visitors realized there was enough going on to keep them entertained beyond the traditional summer season of June through August.

Myrtle Square Mall became a handy central shopping spot, and it had a unique giant clock in its center that became an iconic meeting place for locals. The mall even used the phrase "Meet Me Under the Clock" as part of its advertising.

"The clock was like a big round area," local resident Kathleen Futrell said. "The clock was up in the ceiling; it had lights that would tick off the minutes and so forth. It had benches and things under it…In the center, there [were] seats all around where you could just sit under the clock. Everyone said, 'Meet me at the clock.'"

But Myrtle Square Mall did not make it to the fifty-year mark to have it considered a historic property. It was remodeled in 1985, but then in 2006, the same year Burroughs & Chapin closed the pavilion, Myrtle Square Mall was razed. In the spring of 2014, its site was a barren landscape of sand, grass, concrete and a few trees. The 2009 Horry County Historic Resources

The unique giant clock in the center of Myrtle Square Mall was a favorite meeting spot. *Photo by Ben Schumin.*

Survey says that's going to be the fate of many more vintage structures if the city of Myrtle Beach doesn't implement historic preservation ordinances:

> *Mid-century structures, now reaching the 50-year mark for designation as "historic" are often disregarded for the unusual or plain architecture, aging materials, or because they are located on prime real estate which is encumbered by incompatible zoning. With no comprehensive preservation strategy in place currently for Horry County preservation, it is important to consider several avenues for encouraging the retention of historic sites, including an appeal for tourism, preservation ordinances, and potential incentives for building owners. Commercial sites included in this survey date from the 1890s to the 1960s, many of which display alterations to the façades. There is a concentration of mid-century commercial buildings in Myrtle Beach, Ocean Drive Beach, and Surfside Beach, and early 1900s structures in Loris. Alterations include new siding, replacement of windows and doors, and additions to the structures. Loris and other beach towns do not face the same pressure of development as Myrtle Beach, and few threats*

exist besides the absence of preservation ordinances protecting historic structures. In Myrtle Beach, several groups of historic commercial buildings are still extant, including those along Broadway and the Chapin Building, but with their prime locations, they may fall easily to development pressures. There are currently no ordinances in place to protect these buildings or to place design restrictions on new construction, making it more compatible with the surrounding historic buildings.

THE MYRTLE BEACH PAVILION

The Seaside Inn, built by the sons of F.G. Burroughs and Benjamin Grier Collins in 1901, had Myrtle Beach's first pavilion. There may have been a cruder pavilion built first, but the one most historians note as the first official pavilion was erected in 1908. An elevated wood boardwalk crossed the sand from the hotel to the pavilion, which was in a spot well back from the high tide line. The octagon-shaped pavilion had gray walls with windows in them, white trim and a red roof, which matched the Seaside Inn. A shaded porch where sea breezes cooled the guests in those days predating electricity and air conditioning encircled it. That early pavilion was a social hub where "younger guests waltzed to the pavilion's piano and Victrola," Susan Hoffer McMillan wrote in *Myrtle Beach and the Grand Strand*.

In its own company history book, Burroughs & Chapin says the pavilion was "about midway between the Seaside Inn and the shore, connected by a boardwalk built directly on the sand…it became the social hub of the beach, hosting elegant dances as well as Sunday morning worship services." That first wood pavilion burned down in 1920, and Myrtle Beach Farms built a new one closer to the beach.

"In 1923, Myrtle Beach Farms Co. erected a large, two-story wooden pavilion on the oceanfront," a history note in the December 15, 1999 *Sun News* says. "The pavilion joined the recently constructed boardwalk." It was built "under the supervision of James Bryan Sr.," J. Marcus Smith wrote in 1991, and "the lower [ground] floor had many large archways, which allowed the sea breeze to circulate freely. A concession stand and open dance

In 1923, the new two-story pavilion connected with a wooden boardwalk. *Horry County Museum, Conway, South Carolina.*

area occupied a portion of the floor." Locals of a certain age remember that Myrtle Beach Farms stored produce there in the winter.

A 1925 blurb in the *Florence Morning News* says there was a new orchestra performing at the pavilion. "Buck Capell's orchestra, known as the Carolina Sun Dodgers, has been engaged to play at Myrtle Beach and will open their engagement tonight. After the season at the beach is over the orchestra has arranged dates for several places in Florida."

As noted in an earlier chapter, in 1926 Myrtle Beach Farms sold almost sixty-five thousand acres of land for $950,000 to John T. Woodside of Greenville and his brothers. Woodside built the Ocean Forest Hotel, but the Great Depression reversed his fortunes. In 1933, most of the oceanfront land in the original deal reverted back to ownership with Myrtle Beach Farms.

The 1927 season started with a bang, an item in the June 3, 1927 edition of the *Florence Morning News Review* says: "Plans are all set for the big summer opening here Friday night of this week, starting at 8:30 o'clock with the fireworks display, immediately followed by the grand ball." The pavilion's orchestral band was set to perform for the season, and the band had subgroups of a brass band, a concert orchestra and a jazz band with soloists. A group of bankers was coming to town for a convention, and the article concludes, "Myrtle Beach will doubtless be visited by the greatest crowd in its history so far."

A 1927 pavilion photo shows a long wood structure with arched openings on the ground level that would allow high tides to swell beneath the building.

Windows lined the two tiers of the upper level, with one long windowed side facing the ocean. The pavilion's upper level had a performance stage and a "spacious dance floor," and Smith wrote that there were plenty of rocking chairs for spectators in an area separated from the dancers by a white banister. To the right in the 1927 pavilion photo is a glimpse of another large structure, which author Susan Hoffer McMillan wrote in *Myrtle Beach and the Grand Strand* was a building called the annex. Part of it was used as a dormitory for lifeguards and hired musicians, and it was nicknamed the Bull Pen just like the employees' quarters at the Ocean Forest Hotel would later be named.

When the Ocean Forest Hotel opened in 1930, it brought more visitors to the pavilion. From the first year the hotel opened, professional groups held conventions there, such as the Eastern Carolina Medical Association in July 1930.

The Myrtle Beach Pavilion was entrenched by the time Myrtle Beach Farms regained its thousands of acres from the Woodsides. A 1930 photo shows a shed-like addition along one of its narrow sides with the boardwalk extending under its stilted ground level. "A small, but colorful, carousel occupied the corner of Ninth Avenue and Ocean Boulevard, the site of the present Ripley's Believe It or Not! Museum," J. Marcus Smith wrote in 1991 while recalling his own childhood. "After the summer season owner-operator Robert McMillan stored the merry-go-round in the nearby Blue Sea Inn, operated by the McMillan family for many years."

This postcard, sold at Mack's Five-, Ten- & Twenty-five-cent Stores, depicts "Boardwalk Attractions" at "America's Finest Strand." *Author's collection.*

Smith may have primarily remembered the carousel, as many small children do, but this early pavilion had other amusements around it. Barbara Stokes mentions a 1935 Myrtle Beach promotional brochure that says there was a "midway with a Ferris wheel, carousels, and slides." For several years, an outside firm provided rides on a contract basis with Myrtle Beach Farms before the company started managing them.

In 1943, fire again struck the wood pavilion, and it was rebuilt and enlarged once more. The Myrtle Beach Pavilion reopened in 1948, this time constructed of less flammable and studier materials with brick walls and a poured concrete foundation—the first such foundation in town. The two-story pavilion had a stage for live entertainment, a dance floor, tiered auditorium seating and concessions.

By the time the Myrtle Beach Pavilion was rebuilt, the boardwalk had become more than three thousand feet long and extended both north and south from the pavilion to the farthest oceanfront cottages. The wood part of the boardwalk between the pavilion and the Ocean Plaza Hotel (where the Yachtsman is today at Fourteenth Avenue Pier) was replaced in 1940 by a twelve-foot-wide concrete sidewalk. "Plans were made to extend the concrete walk the entire length of the seven-mile beach front," Smith wrote. "With the advent of World War II, the beachfront project stopped. The remainder of the wooden boardwalk was maintained, but it slowly deteriorated."

THE CAROUSEL AND THE ORGAN

While the early pavilions were all about dancing and socializing, as time progressed, the site expanded to include amusements. When Kathleen Macklen Futrell started working there as a young teenager in the late 1940s, it had become an amusement park. Soon it was enhanced with a 1912 carousel and a circa 1900 German Baden Band Organ.

The Herschell-Spillman Company built the pavilion's carousel in 1912 in North Tonawanda, New York. The company built four other carousels at the same time, Blanche Floyd wrote in 1991, and the only one left in use is in Myrtle Beach. It is one of fifteen similar carousels still in existence. A sign that used to stand near the carousel's covered open-air building at the Myrtle Beach Pavilion said it was purchased and brought to Myrtle Beach in the spring of 1950 from Billy Morgan's Oxford Lake Park in Anniston, Alabama. All but two of its animals were hand-carved by the Herschell-

The Herschell-Spillman carousel shown in this 1955 advertisement was brought to the pavilion in 1950. *Author's collection.*

Spillman Company. The two exceptions are the paired elephants dated 1890 that were made by U.S. Carousel.

The classic wood carousel has entertained generations of children since then with its fifty glossy and intricately carved and painted country fair–style animals rising up and down while its three tiered levels spin in circles. It has horses with armored and beribboned heads and a storybook fantasy menagerie filled with a colorful and elaborately decorated pair of giraffes, one bejeweled tiger, a goat, two roosters, a tassel-draped camel, two dogs, two cats, one lion with an impressive mane, a stork, two zebras and one pig with a ribbon around its neck and another trotting off with a cornstalk in its mouth. A vividly blue sea dragon has a gold mane, pink tongue and sharp talons. The Neptune's Chariot bench seat is where parents can sit and hold lap babies as music plays gaily and the ride whirls.

In the carousel's center is an electric Wurlitzer organ. A rounding board above the central motor displays more animals with vintage circus flair. Four of its horses have been depicted on postage stamps, Floyd wrote in 1991.

"The late Earl Husted, who for years served as general manager of the Pavilion, said in an interview some years ago that he valued the carousel at a million dollars, and even at that it could not be replaced."

The Ruth & Sohn Company in Germany built the German Baden Band Organ for the 1900 Paris World Exposition, and it found a home at the Myrtle Beach Pavilion in 1954. There were benches in front of the organ at the pavilion where people sat and listened to its automated music, which is similar to that from a player piano but much louder and grander. The Myrtle Beach Comprehensive Plan contains more details about the band organ:

> It was originally constructed for the World Exposition in Paris, France, and was featured as the main attraction. After the World Exposition, it was shipped back to Germany where it traveled from town to town, being used for different entertainment events, in a wagon led by a team of six horses. Twenty years later, the organ was purchased by a wealthy American industrialist who placed the organ in a room he had specially built on his estate in Martha's Vineyard, Massachusetts. The organ remained in Martha's Vineyard for thirty years where friends and family as well as musicians and bandleaders enjoyed it. In the 1950s, Mr. Harry Beach of Myrtle Beach Farms Company went to Martha's Vineyard to try to buy the organ. The organ was shipped to Myrtle Beach in 1954 and has been in the Pavilion Amusement Park since that time. The organ is 11 feet high, 20 feet long and 7 feet deep. It weighs about two tons. Working parts include 400 pipes with 98 keys, and 18 life-like hand-carved figures. These figures include 12 that move in rhythm to the music, 2 of which play the harp and others that beat drums. The organ was originally operated by hand, featuring a large wheel that had to be manually turned to channel air through the machine. The hand-turned wheel has since been replaced by a motor, which compresses the air electrically.

Joyce Herian, who grew up on a farm in western Horry County, says the organ and carousel stand out as fond childhood memories from the trips they made to the beach two or three times a year. "The music and the great organ that we had—it made you so happy to listen to that music in the background as you'd go from one ride to another. Later on, I always thought that was such a big treat in my life when my kids came along."

The organ and carousel were briefly on the National Register of Historic Places, but they were removed by the owner's request, the 2009 Horry County Historic Resources Survey says. As of the spring of 2014, they had been relocated to Broadway at the Beach, a dining/entertainment/shopping complex owned by Burroughs & Chapin. It's a few blocks inland and several blocks north of the former Myrtle Beach Pavilion.

OTHER RIDES AND ENTERTAINMENT

In early years, the pavilion was the site of fireworks, but beginning in 1984, they were canceled when the state fire marshal prohibited "fireworks within 600 feet of buildings, crowds, roads or trees."

Jack Bourne remembers an organ grinder's monkey:

> *Everybody would be in a big circle. And that guy would be grinding out the music, and the monkey would dance. People would hold out their money—a nickel, dime—and the monkey would go around and take it from you and tip his hat and then go over and give it to the grinder. You could hold a penny out there for five minutes, and he wouldn't come to you…That guy had him trained to get silver money. He wouldn't even mess with you for a penny.*

Games of chance were fun ways to try to spend a little money to get a prize. Over the decades, they included Skee-Ball, penny pitching, water gun races and dozens of other midway-type games that could part people from a few coins and leave some of them thrilled to carry home a stuffed animal or pavilion logo item.

Rides changed through the years. There were bumper cars and plenty of rides for tiny children, like little boats that went around in circles in a pool of water. The Comet was the pavilion's first roller coaster in 1950, and its cars had a futuristic space theme. In the mid-1980s, the pavilion had two roller coasters: the Galaxie had two spirals, one at each end, while the Corkscrew had loop-the-loops and was a brief ride. The Corkscrew came from another local amusement park called Magic Harbor. In 1984, a log flume was introduced.

A double Ferris wheel was later replaced by a taller single "Big Eli" Ferris wheel. In 1991, a seventeen-year-old boy from Wilmington died when he fell forty feet from one of the cabs. His twelve-year-old sister also fell, and as they were falling, they hit another cab, which caused two more children to fall. One of the children became entangled in the ride so that rescue personnel had to use a "sky ladder" to rescue her. The ride was four years old when the

In the 1950s, Donnie King (left) and Tilman Mishoe had a souvenir photo taken at the Myrtle Beach Pavilion. *Peggy Mishoe collection.*

Servicemen from the Myrtle Beach Army Air Base mingled with tourists at the Myrtle Beach Pavilion. *Cooper collection, Horry County Museum, Conway, South Carolina.*

accident happened; a friend riding in the cab with the Wilmington children said they had been rocking the car before it flipped over. The Big Eli was subsequently removed from the park.

The pavilion had miniature golf, a baseball batting cage, a Tilt-a-Whirl, a haunted house, fun mirrors, fountains in animal statues, photo booths where you could dress up in Wild West clothing and swings that flung its riders in smooth and speedy circles.

In the 1990s, even more thrilling rides were added, like the Hydro Surge, where people sat in chairs on a raft in a circle facing one another and rode simulated white water rapids. It was an excellent ride when the weather was hot and you wanted to cool off, but it wasn't so much fun on chilly days. The Top Spin had people sitting in long rows that spun like a Ferris wheel while flipping riders upside down.

A splashy addition to the staple rides in 2000 was the Hurricane roller coaster, a $5 million custom coaster with a fifty-five-mile-per-hour, one-hundred-foot drop that replaced the Corkscrew. The Gravitron used centrifugal force to keep riders against the walls while the floor dropped out, while the Pirate Ship was a huge ship that rocked ever higher back and forth until its riders could look out over the ocean.

Seeing the ocean from atop the rides was an integral part of the appeal. The Myrtle Beach Pavilion was known worldwide to generations of families as an old-fashioned amusement park by the sea.

HUMAN SPECTACLE

The entire time the pavilion was open, outside entertainment acts were brought in. Kathleen Futrell recalls high wire acts and wrestling bouts. One wrestler in particular who she remembers was a "famous lady wrestler" from Columbia, South Carolina, with the stage name Slave Girl Moolah.

Lillian Ellison (1923–2007) was her real name, and it was in the 1940s and early '50s that the tiny woman—five feet, four inches and 118 pounds—wrestled as Slave Girl Moolah in her signature leopard-print and jungle girl costumes. Her onstage persona was wicked, and the crowds loved to hate her. Although Ellison's wrestling circuit travels took her to many cities throughout the United States, Columbia was home base for most of her life.

In 1956, her named changed by then to the Fabulous Moolah, Ellison won the women's wrestling championship belt. After New York lifted a ban on women's wrestling in 1972, she was the first woman to have a match there. Moolah won that day, and she held the title of Women's Wrestling Champion for twenty-eight years and then won her championship belt back again at age seventy-six.

An act that came to the pavilion in 1955 was Princess Tall Chief. An advertisement said, "Throbbing Indian rhythms and breath-taking body control of this Iroquois Princess will charm you." Another ad billed her as an "acrobatic novelty act."

The high wire act Kathleen Futrell remembers is likely the Flying Wallendas, a family of traveling aerialists who performed regularly at the pavilion for decades. A 1976 article in the *Sarasota Herald-Tribune* says the famous troupe's founder, Karl Wallenda, spent that summer performing at the pavilion with his family of daredevil entertainers who were famous for not using nets.

Another well-known trapeze artist who performed at the pavilion was Norma Fox, who was known as La Norma. A native of Denmark, she enthralled crowds with her one-toe hanging while performing with the Ringling Brothers Barnum & Bailey Circus and the Clyde Beatty–Cole Brothers Circus. In 1952, Fox was the stunt double for Betty Hutton in the Cecil B. DeMille movie starring James Stewart called *The Greatest Show on Earth*.

But in 1969, while performing in Myrtle Beach, Norma Fox fell, as detailed in a *Sarasota Herald-Tribune* article:

> *Mrs. Fox was performing at a seaside amusement park in Myrtle Beach, S.C., in 1969 when a 75-foot fall almost ended her career at age 41. She*

LOST MYRTLE BEACH

AT THE PAVILLION

Princess Tall Chief

DISTANCES
From Myrtle Beach
South

State Park	3	Miles
Surfside	8	Miles
Garden City	11	Miles
Murrell's Inlet	13	Miles
Pawley's Island	22	Miles
Georgetown	34	Miles

Princess Tall Chief was one of the traveling acts that came to the pavilion in 1955. *Author's collection.*

was performing on a trapeze attached to a mechanical rigging that simulated a rocket and satellite orbiting the earth. Her husband, Andre Fox, a former circus horse rider and trainer, built and operated the impressively large machinery. The equipment was supported with guidewires attached to stakes driven in the sand. Mrs. Fox recalls being uneasy about the looseness of the sand, because it had just been poured on the beach as a restoration project. She was making a final swing on the trapeze at the close of a performance when a stake pulled out and the heavy machinery collapsed on top of her, pounding her body into the sand as her husband stood helpless at the control panel. Mrs. Fox broke her collar bones, her back, ribs, pelvis and caved in her face.

Seven months later, she was performing again.

Myrtle Beach native Mike McKinnon remembers seeing a "wild" motorcycle high wire act. Johnny Butler also recalls the spectacle:

They had wrassling upstairs. A big wrassling ring was set up that was at times a skating rink and rock-and-roll show. It was the coolest thing. They had what we would call professional wrestling. The standout was a little old guy about four [feet], five [inches and one] hundred pounds. Haystack Calhoun was the featured wrassler, and they would have tag team bouts on Saturday nights. Back then, they had the [Flying] Wallendas outside right on the little cul-de-sac right there on the beach. We'd go down there at nighttime, and we'd have French fries with vinegar all over [them and] candy apples and watch the Flying Wallendas. They came in the summertime, about once a month. They staggered the acts that they had. One guy would jump off a high dive into a foot of water. In wintertime, upstairs in the Attic, they would convert to a roller skating rink. We had a huge time. All the people I went to school with, on Friday, Saturday, Sunday afternoons, that's where we were. It was a huge time, the simplicity of things...I understand now and have for a long time—my friends and I know how lucky we are to grow up in that timeframe and to have been raised in Myrtle Beach. It was such a treat.

CITY IDENTITY

Kathleen Macklen Futrell was born in 1935, and she still lives in the Socastee home where her father was born. She says the pavilion was an important part of her life. She visited it as a child, and when she was in ninth grade in 1949, she started working there, selling concessions. After graduating fromhigh school, Futrell continued working at the pavilion during college summer breaks, and after college at the University of South Carolina, Futrell became a physical education and science teacher in Columbia for two years and then taught for the remainder of her career at Socastee High School until she retired in the late 1970s. Every summer during her teaching career and into retirement through 1988, Futrell worked all summer at the pavilion. Eventually, her employer changed from Myrtle Beach Farms to working for an independent contractor named Don Husted, and then she went into business with Husted before buying him out and owning her pavilion concession outright. In total, she worked at the pavilion for forty summers. She recalled her time there:

> I don't remember the first wooden building that was there, but I know when they built the second wooden building when I was a child. They had a skating rink up in the top…I was in Myrtle Beach of course when it burned, and they built the next pavilion in about 1948, '49…It was a big wooden building with open big archways and whatever, and the skating rink and things like that. There might have been some rides over on the waterfront…The crowds were tremendous. It was the place to go, and it was just totally different from the way it got to be at the end. They had benches out there along the ocean side and everywhere. People would bring their kids and ride the rides and sit there and watch the ocean. It was child-friendly. You didn't have to worry about your kids being around or by themselves or anything back then, and the parents would just come and sit and talk and enjoy themselves with the others. The amusement park was across the street, and they did real well. It was the only thing like it at the beach, so of course when the tourists came that was their destination. They had parking along between the pavilion and the rides, and they would sit in their cars and there were no parking meters. It was just nice…fifteen dollars a week was my paycheck in 1949. That was so much; no other kid around had that much money. You could take that money and go to the grill at the pavilion and pay twenty cent for a hot dog and a nickel for a drink. They gave employees a special rate.

Barbara Horner's family is from the mountains of North Carolina, and her family has owned property in the Seventy-sixth Avenue North area of Myrtle Beach since about 1940. She remembers spending summer vacations in Myrtle Beach with extended family. Lee's Inlet Kitchen in Murrells Inlet was her father's favorite restaurant: "I remember we would always go there for dinner and then, in the middle of the day, spend the afternoon at the pavilion. We were hardly ever there at night…Usually it opened at two, and the rides would go on until about ten o'clock at night. And then the town closed up; everybody left."

Ann Vereen's pavilion memories started in the late 1940s:

> *The pavilion was so fantastic. The floor shows were what we lived for. They had all kinds of entertainment. You went upstairs…and they had variety shows and just all kinds of things before the actual dances started up there…I remember the artists doing acrobatics—the Flying Wallendas, those kinds of people…We were turned loose as children to walk all the way to the pavilion, ten or twelve blocks, but it was no problem. We knew the people between where we lived and the pavilion…I remember when they brought the organ—that was so wonderful.*

Johnny Butler, who grew up near Withers Swash, remembers visiting the pavilion in the 1950s:

> *When I was a kid, the amusement park was very simple. They closed the back street in and expanded the park out when I was a teenager. In the early days, it had a Big Eli Ferris Wheel, the old pipe organ, the merry-go-round. There was just excitement in the air…The deal was on Monday you'd get twelve tickets in a book for a dollar. Back then, it took one ticket to ride one ride. Later, it took three tickets and so on…Kids were running around and exciting things were going on.*

In the 1960s, when Butler was a teenager, he and most of his friends worked summers at the pavilion. Edgerton Burroughs, who grew up to sit on the board of directors of Burroughs & Chapin, worked at the bumper cars ride. Marshall McMillan, who became the treasurer at Burroughs & Chapin, worked in the Attic. Butler said they had fun:

> *I was just getting into the shag thing and understanding what the shag music was. We had a jukebox that sat over by the flagpole, by the over-walk at the pavilion. The jukebox was sitting inside a big wood cabinet. At eight o'clock in the evening, the rock-and-roll show would start with the Catalinas. They would come and lock the jukebox up; they would turn it off. They wanted you to come upstairs and pay the admission fee for the rock-and-roll show. I would*

get a foot-long hot dog when I could get a quarter together. I always checked the coin return, and if I found a quarter, that would be my hot dog for the day. As an employee, I didn't have to pay to get into the show. Me and Skeeter Nash, Rock Smith, we'd be up [at] the rock-and-roll show trying to meet little old girls. We'd be up there until midnight dancing.

Dancing was a major pastime at the pavilion until the park was destroyed. For more than one hundred years, that piece of beach witnessed practically every popular American dance, from ballroom dancing to the lindy to jitterbugging, which evolved into the shag. In more modern times, the oceanfront pavilion building had an upstairs teen club called the Magic Attic.

Myrtle Beach chefs Mike McKinnon and Billy Wright remember picking up vacationing girls at Dunes Village, a horseshoe-shape hotel at Fifty-second Avenue North, and taking them to the Magic Attic. If they couldn't get a date before hitting the Attic, they'd try to hook up with girls there. Wright remembers someone asking if he was going to enter a breakdance competition. "I'd say, 'Hell yeah, I can.' I didn't know how to breakdance. Still don't. You know, just to get the girls, you get up on stage—the place is packed—and then get booed off the stage, but [you] still get the girl."

In addition to working as an executive chef, Wright is a musician. During high school, he was in a band called Uncle Wonderful that, in 1988, played its first gig at the Magic Attic. He and McKinnon remember Mother's Finest playing there, and Sugarcreek out of Charlotte was a longtime favorite. Tim Clark, the lead singer for Sugarcreek, eventually moved to Myrtle Beach and opened his own nightclub. Later, the magic left the teen nightclub, and it was called simply the Attic.

In the late 1960s and early '70s, McKinnon remembers riding his bicycle and skateboard all around town, including through the middle of the pavilion. It wasn't allowed; he was chased out. During that period, the pavilion still had a bathhouse where people could change clothes.

Karon Bowers Jones recalls there being brick walls around the pavilion when she was a child in the 1960s. Later, the walls were torn down, and a family friend used some of those bricks to build a house on Pine Lakes Drive in Myrtle Beach.

Before integration, African Americans were not allowed to even buy an ice cream cone at the pavilion. Desegregation of Myrtle Beach schools happened in 1965, and after that, people who lived in the nearby black communities just blocks from the pavilion—close enough to hear the music and the crowds—could share in the fun.

THE ANNOUNCEMENT

Johnny Butler, who was the pavilion's food and beverage manager, remembers when staff managers were told the pavilion would be open for only one more season. They were called to a meeting in the office of Burroughs & Chapin president and CEO Doug Wendel. Butler recalled:

> *We had no clue they were going to close. We're all sitting there with our mouths gaped wide open. He didn't give us a reason. It wasn't none of our business. It was a decision* [made] *by the shareholders, and that's what we did…Revenue-wise, 2006 was the best year in the history of the pavilion. Revenue had not been falling off before that. It would be slight increases, not huge…They would say that they wanted to use the land for other things. Wanted to come in with timeshares or a hotel. I didn't ever kind of believe that. I think there was something that obviously didn't materialize later on.*

That final season, locals and tourists who visited the pavilion for decades poured into the park. A special "farewell season" logo was made, and special events and promotions were scheduled throughout the summer.

Barbara Horner was working at the *Sun News* as an archivist when the final season announcement was made. "I think we all sat down and cried," she said. "I remember it being a really sad occasion. Everybody looked at each other; we couldn't believe it [and said] 'It won't happen, they won't do that, they won't tear it down.' But it was a very sad occasion." Horner said anger was mixed in with the sadness she and her co-workers felt: "It was so secretive; nobody knew why. Nobody knew they were going to do it until it started happening. And I guess I had the inner circle because I was at the *Sun News*, and I knew then that it was going to happen. I think even the *Sun News* was sort of sad about it."

Horner took her sons and grandchildren to the pavilion on its final day of operation, and she remembers bulldozers were already lined up and ready to begin demolition.

"Oh, we were so sad," Ann Vereen said. "My girlfriends and I went down, and on like the last week, we rode all the rides. We didn't know we could still do that, but we did…Even at our age, we had to go do it. We just walked and walked and went over to Peaches Corner and ate malted French fries. We were so upset about it."

When it was announced the pavilion would be torn down, Karon Bowers Jones had moved to California. She remembers the day in December 2006 when bulldozers arrived at the site:

I was just in awe. I mean, I was like, I cannot believe this—this is it. I know you want to tear down landmarks because things need to be built, but this was something that brought a lot of people to Myrtle Beach. I mean, that was the big thing. And I was just [thinking], *"What is Burroughs & Chapin*

Ashton Fowler of Conway (rear) was joined by her brother, Logan Fowler, and sister, Reagan Fowler, during the final season at the Myrtle Beach Pavilion. *Photo by Russell Fowler.*

thinking?"....I went away from the computer and went about my business, and every time I would come back into my room where my computer was, I would pull that picture up again. It showed a bulldozer, and I was just crazy. I mean, it was just like somebody had stabbed me in the back.

Patrick Killian, Jesse Sawyer and Chris Henderson, who were born between 1989 and 1993, belong to the last generation to remember visiting the pavilion. Their families had season passes, and the rides are vivid parts of their childhood memories.

"[The pavilion] provided something; it was the beach's own," Sawyer said. "The pavilion was Myrtle Beach. That was downtown Myrtle Beach—the pavilion and the boardwalk, that section of the boulevard."

"I just couldn't believe it had closed," Henderson said. "It had been open for so long. It was like a historical landmark in front of Myrtle Beach."

Killian and Sawyer's final memory of the pavilion is a momentous one. They were seventeen years old during the final season, and their ska band, the Bottlecap Bandits, performed there. They got to see the band's name in lights, as did many other local musicians from generations before them.

A Hollywood-style walk of fame for local and visiting celebrities was on the sidewalk in front of the pavilion. When the park was closed, they were removed.

The 2009 Horry County Historic Resource Survey says:

The demolition of the Pavilion amusement park in early 2007 sparked a loud outcry from Myrtle Beach citizens and visitors alike, prompting the local newspaper to solicit written and photographic memorabilia. The loss of the Pavilion is a significant change to the character of the town, and will have far reaching effects, perhaps one of the most important being the introduction of a large scale building further inland from the beach, where most high rises now exist, and its subsequent overshadowing of surrounding mid-century buildings and hotels.

11

SUN FUN FESTIVAL

The Myrtle Beach Sun Fun Festival was conceived in 1951 as a way to get families within easy driving distance to come to the beach to celebrate the end of school. Held for four days during the first full weekend in June, it provided a jump-start for seasonal Grand Strand business owners.

Myrtle Beach Sun newspaper publisher and chamber of commerce president Mark Garner chaired the first festival in 1951. Eventually, the festival spread throughout the Grand Strand area to include events from North Myrtle Beach to Surfside Beach, and civic organizations pitched in to organize everything.

In 2004, Harold Clardy (1927–2012), who was president of the Chapin Company department store and was heavily involved in organizing Sun Fun Festivals, recalled how it started and evolved.

The first Sun Fun event didn't have a proper name, Clardy remembered—that didn't come until 1952, when June Truluck won twenty-five dollars for submitting the winning name—but everyone knew they had a hit on their hands. People came in droves for the casual beach excitement.

"At the first Sun Fun, we did something out of the ordinary," Clardy said at age seventy-seven. "We had a Sun Fun jail. If you didn't wear shorts on Sun Fun day, you had to go to the Sun Fun jail; so that drew a little attention…I never did get locked up, because I paid the fine to keep from going to jail. The Sun Fun Police were pretty girls, the beauty queens." In those early days of the official Sun Fun Festival, fines paid to get out of jail were donated to Ocean View Memorial Hospital.

Beautiful women were already synonymous with sun and fun in Myrtle Beach. A 1939 article in the *Aiken Standard and Review* details the official launch of the summer season on May 30 when South Carolina senator James F. Byrnes came to town to give an "address at the official opening of the Ocean Forest Hotel and the Washington Park race track." The hotel was holding an annual golf tournament that day for southern sports writers, and the Ocean Forest was also the site that day for a Bathing Beauty Luncheon. As in later years when the festival was formally established, many Myrtle Beach civic organizations took part in the festivities of that day including, "Legion and Auxillary, Civitans, Lions, Masons, Parents and Teachers [and the] Chamber of Commerce."

Kathleen Futrell of Myrtle Beach remembers the first Sun Fun Festival because she was selling snow cones and ice cream at the pavilion.

She said in November 2013:

> *It was a big thing at one time. The parade always came by the pavilion. They even had the Miss South Carolina contest upstairs in the pavilion for several years before it moved to other areas…They did human checkers [games] right out on the beach. I could see it from my concession stand…A lot of tourists would come that week to participate in Sun Fun activities. North Myrtle Beach, Surfside Beach, they all had something going on constantly, every hour, all week. Checkers, dance contests, watermelon-eating contests, all kinds of games and contests for the children.*

From 1952 through 1957, Clardy said, the Sun Fun Festival hosted the Miss South Carolina pageant. The Myrtle Beach Jaycees had the event's franchise rights for eight years, but in 1958, it moved to Greenville, where those Jaycees "offered Textile Hall, TV coverage and more adequate facilities," local historian and optometrist J. Marcus Smith (1925–2008) wrote in 1995.

Those early days also featured bathing beauties and surfing hunks as the pieces on a human-size checkers board and as beach volleyball teammates. Ann Vereen, who was born in Conway in 1943, remembers the fun.

"Sun Fun was grand," she said. "That was such a special week, especially coming over and being put in 'jail.' If you didn't have shorts you were put in jail, so it was a big deal. If we were in school, we would absolutely try to cut school to get over here. We did not want to miss Sun Fun."

The *Loris Sentinel* published an article in 1953 about the upcoming Sun Fun Festival. Events that year featured motorboat races and a jousting tournament sponsored by the Rotary Club. The Myrtle Beach Elks Club sponsored the Sun Fun jail that year. "Arrests will be made by the world's prettiest cops and costumes ranging from Bikini to the old fashioned bathing suits will be seen," the article says. Celebrities expected to attend were Mickey Spillane, Hugh Morton, Orville Campbell and B.H. Frapar. A treasure hunt was held with the winner finding a prize worth "at least $50" hidden on the beach.

More events at the 1953 Sun Fun Festival were the baton twirling state finals and a press photo contest for the best picture of Miss South Carolina (prizes were $25, $50 and $100), "To close the 1953 Sun-Fun Festival," the article says, "all of the Queens will attend church together Sunday morning." That year, *Look Magazine* ran an article about the festival with its own photos by Jim Hansen (1921–1999), and locals were excited about the high-profile national coverage.

According to climatological data published by the U.S. Weather Bureau, a rain deluge marred the 1954 Sun Fun Festival:

> *A record heavy rainfall occurred at Conway, S.C., on the Waccamaw River on [June] 6th–7th. A total of 10.38 inches was recorded in 14 hours and 30 minutes. The return period for such a 24-hour rainfall at this station would be 100 years. Heavy flash flooding occurred in the urban and rural areas of this community. Large segments of Horry County were isolated and thousands of vacationers enroute [sic] to and from Myrtle Beach, S.C., for the Sun Fun Festival on the Grand Strand were halted for many hours. Heavily traveled U.S. Highways 701, 501, 378, and several lesser used roadways were blocked off. About 2 feet of water accumulated in the main street of Conway. Several cars were swept from U.S. 501 by the flash flood before the road could be closed off.*

In 1956, the Myrtle Beach Chamber of Commerce promoted the festival with an advertisement in the Charleston, West Virginia *Gazette*. "The Riviera of the South," it says. "Gala days await you at the Sun-Fun Festival…a summer mardi gras!" Attendees could expect to help choose Miss South Carolina, meet Miss America, play games, participate in contests, watch a "fabulous parade with gorgeous girls and flower-laden floats," dance in the streets in masquerade attire and "tee off on two excellent golf courses."

The Sun Fun Festival held June 5–9, 1957, was noteworthy because the Myrtle Beach Army Air Base, "opened its doors to the public," Smith wrote. He said also of the 1957 festival:

City officials designated Thursday as Sun Fun Day and issued a proclamation requiring all inhabitants to wear beach attire, bathing suits or shorts between dawn and noon in downtown Myrtle Beach. Festival lady cops quickly arrested violators and escorted them to the Sun Fun Court, where they were tried and sentenced by Father Neptune. Guilty culprits landed in "Davy Jones' locker" (Sun Fun Jail). Among the inmates were Mickey Spillane, beauty contestants and local dignitaries. Mermaids collected the $1 fine and placed the money in a sea chest for local charities. The festival "slammer" stood in front of the small frame chamber of commerce building on the east side of Kings Highway, near Ninth Avenue North.

Smith described how the Ocean Forest Hotel sponsored a public "dancing under the stars" event at its Marine Patio, and the hotel also had a members-only Masquerader's Ball to commemorate Sun Fun.

In 1958, a new racetrack opened five miles west of Myrtle Beach off U.S. 501, and the 1959 Sun Fun Festival had "six turf events featuring thoroughbred horses," Barbara Stokes wrote. In 1960, the racetrack hosted the "third annual Sports Car Gymkana," where some fifty drivers participated in "an obstacle race against time." Also in 1960, a casting tournament was held at the Myrtle Beach High School football field. "The casting tourney will also coincide with the opening of the 1960 $6,000 Grand Strand Fishing Rodeo," an article in the Charleston, West Virginia *Gazette-Mail* said. "The Fishing Rodeo covers a 50-mile area of the South Carolina Coast."

The Sun Fun USA Pageant was one of the many bathing beauty titles at the festival, and in 1960, the winner was Darlene Lucht (1937–2011) of Milwaukee, Wisconsin. She won "four trips, jewelry, and a 1960 Corvair...Also included were a dinner with U.S. Senator Strom Thurmond and a half-hour interview with WRC-TV where she provided free advertising for Myrtle Beach," according to a 2009 dissertation by Richard R. Hourigan III.

Chamber of commerce employees used these bathing beauties to promote Myrtle Beach. The 1963 Sun Fun USA queen, Ginger Poitevint, was sent to New York to appear on the TV game show *To Tell the Truth*. "After the shooting, she raced up to the top of the Empire State Building where she helped build a castle made of sand from Myrtle Beach," Hourigan wrote.

A fictional 1963 Sun Fun Festival was portrayed in the 1989 film called *Shag: The Movie*. The movie's main character, a teenage girl, plans to win the bathing beauty pageant so a fictional Sun Fun celebrity named Jimmy Valentine will fall in love with her.

Miss Teen Sun Fun Mary Grace Dallery of Sumter on left and Miss Sun Fun Katie Brown of Spartanburg were named the final Miss Sun Funs in 2011 before the Myrtle Beach Area Chamber of Commerce canceled the Sun Fun Festival in 2012. *Photo by Matt Silfer, Silfer Studios.*

Miss America Desree Jenkins visited the festival in 1965, but there was no beauty contest because the Miss Sun Fun USA pageant was suspended after 1964. In 1965, "a big criticism of the Sun Fun festival was the lack of a beauty pageant and two days of rain," according to a 1990 *Sun News* history column.

It was not until 2005 that the Miss Sun Fun USA title returned, and it was a preliminary event to the Miss USA pageant. A Miss Teen Sun Fun USA title was also part of the event, which was held annually through 2011. However, instead of taking place downtown in Myrtle Beach as in years past, the new Miss Sun Fun USA pageant was held at different area high schools.

Through the years, some entertainment remained constant—like bathing beauties participating in events most years and many wholesome children's events such as watermelon-eating contests—but new twists kept things interesting. In 1966, the festival had a Wild West theme (perhaps to coincide with the new Fort Caroline amusement park west of town) complete with a sand-building contest, where instead of castles, participants constructed teepees and frontier forts. Also that year, the parade was postponed due to Hurricane Alma.

THE PARADE

The Sun Fun Parade was a centerpiece of the long weekend. The parade was Harold Clardy's specialty because he was a member of the Myrtle Beach Lions Club, and for many years, they were the folks in charge of handling organization details on parade day.

"There were probably twenty to twenty-five groups in that first parade," he said, "plus the bands. Later, we had the military bands coming in. When the Myrtle Beach Air Force base came into existence in the 1960s, we had more military participation."

In 1953, the parade started at 2:30 p.m. "Floats are being procured by the Lions Club and local floats will be built and decorated by the Garden Club and Pilots Club," a *Loris Sentinel* article said. "The parade will be under the direction of the American Legion. Bands from Parris Island Marine Base, Ninth Air Force, Myrtle Beach High School, Mullins High School, Shallotte High School and others will be entered. Visiting bands are being fed by the Myrtle Beach Restaurant Association."

Locals recall Sun Fun parades lasting up to three and a half hours; J. Marcus Smith wrote that the 1957 parade was a mile long.

Karon Bowers Jones loved the parades and said:

> *I remember as a child sitting on the sides, the Shriners always throwing out candy and getting that* [candy]. *And being hot because it was three and a half hours long…I remember my mom, when we would go down, she would make sure that she had* [a basket]…*and she'd make sure that we had Cokes and snacks and a little sandwich because it took so long—because it started at ten and didn't finish until one, and by the time you'd get home, it was like two o'clock…It just went on and on and on, and* [there were] *people from all over. I mean, it would be like people in Georgia would be coming in, and they would be performing in the parade…*[Nine out of ten] *of the people that sat on the left-hand side* [of the street] *were all the locals, and the right-*

The Sun Fun Parade was known to last three and a half hours. *Horry County Museum, Conway, South Carolina.*

hand side were the visitors. And I think that the home people out-did the visitors…It was a big to-do.

Four days before the Sun Fun Festival Parade in 1967, the Wilmington, North Carolina *Star-News* gave advance information in an article titled "Big Parade Highlight of Sun Fun Festival." It described how the parade was going to be two miles long and would coincide with the world premiere at the Rivoli Theatre in Myrtle Beach of the MGM movie *Don't Make Waves*, a beach party movie starring Tony Curtis, Claudia Cardinale, Sharon Tate, Edgar Bergen and Jim Backus.

The U.S. Army's Golden Knights skydiving team performed, which had a connection to *Don't Make Waves*. The movie had a skydiving sequence that made news because it was shot during thirty-five parachute jumps using a helmet camera.

The 1967 parade was scheduled to have "21 high school bands from five states, 37 elaborate floats and scores of pretty girls, including festival queens from four states. They will be viewed by an estimated 150,000 visitors," according to the Wilmington *Star-News*.

Military personnel from the Myrtle Beach Air Force Base and the U.S. Army had high profiles in the 1967 festival. A new display that year

The world premiere of *Don't Make Waves*, starring Tony Curtis, happened during the 1967 Sun Fun Festival at the Rivoli Theatre. *Author's collection.*

Actress Sharon Tate came to Myrtle Beach for the premiere of *Don't Make Waves*, and she participated in poolside Sun Fun Festival activities. *Horry County Museum, Conway, South Carolina.*

was a sixty-five-foot-long Minuteman intercontinental ballistic missile, which the article said was "currently the mainstay of America's nuclear delivery force, with more than 800 missiles in place throughout the northern section of the United States." Jet aircraft on display were an F-100 Super Sabre, an RF-101 Voodoo, an F-105 Thunderchief, an RF-4C Phantom II, an RB-66 jet bomber, an HH-43B Huskie helicopter, an F-102A Delta Dagger interceptor and a T-33 jet trainer. The jet fighters were flown during the festival to "demonstrate [their] high and low speed characteristics."

In 1985, Ann Vereen got up at 4:00 a.m. so she could meet that year's parade grand marshal, NBC *Today Show* weatherman Willard Scott. "We miss that, the parade," she said. "We went out early so we could get a good seat. I remember the pretty cars and the floats and always some movie star who was going to be a grand marshal."

By 2004, when Harold Clardy was interviewed, the parade was limited to one hundred entries to keep roads from being tied up for no longer than two hours.

Michelle Johnson Householder grew up in Myrtle Beach in the 1970s and '80s. Her grandmother Murrell Allen had the Myrtle Beach Sewing Shop on Eighth Avenue North, and she made the white satin monogrammed sashes worn by Sun Fun beauty contestants.

Ann Vereen of Myrtle Beach got up at 4:00 a.m. in June 1985 to meet that year's Sun Fun Parade grand marshal, weatherman Willard Scott. *Ann Vereen collection.*

"Grandmother [and I] made the banner sashes," Householder said in November 2013. "We monogrammed the front—they were white satin—and sewed the fringe on. I absolutely loved the Sun Fun Festival. I'd see the parade, girls on the floats with their festival banners on. I'd put the banners on and prance around the shop [and pretend to be] Miss Sun Fun, Miss Bikini Wahine."

Householder remembers the Sun Fun Parade passing right in front of the shop and how she and her family and friends eagerly awaited learning which national celebrity would be the Sun Fun Parade grand marshal.

"We just couldn't wait to find out who the grand marshal was going to be," she said. "We were watching the papers and announcements weeks and weeks ahead of time. Some of my favorite [grand marshals] would be a lot of cast members from *General Hospital*. Michael Damian came—he played on *The Young and the Restless*."

Sun Fun Parade grand marshals through the years included a wide variety of celebrities. At the twenty-fifth Sun Fun in 1976, which had a bicentennial theme, Bob Keeshan (Captain Kangaroo) was the grand marshal of twin parades in Myrtle Beach and North Myrtle Beach. Other years, grand marshals were Larry Manetti of the television show *Magnum P.I.* (1987); Vanna White of *Wheel of Fortune*, who grew up in North Myrtle Beach (2001); John Boy and Billy (2005); and Miss USA 2005, Chelsea Cooley, in 2006, which was the final year of an official Sun Fun Parade.

In 1985, festival organizers added a sports grand marshal to the parade, and that year, it was former Clemson University quarterback and basketball player Mike Eppley. Sun Fun concert performers through the years have included Bob Dylan, Willie Nelson, Jordin Sparks and David Archuletta.

Many local businesses and organizations benefitted from the Sun Fun long weekend. In 1967, the Sun Fun Festival was named one of the top twenty June travel events in the United States by the National Association of Travel Organizations. In 1969, the newly formed Waccamaw Arts and Crafts Guild "planned its first sidewalk art show during the Sun Fun Festival," according to a May 1994 history column in the *Sun News*. Another history column from May 1993 noted that in June 1968, "the Sun Fun Festival got under way with the first East Coast surfers meet, a dance on Chester Street in front of the Rivoli Theater and the largest skeet shoot in the East."

One of the premier Sun Fun events locals anticipated was flying demonstrations from the U.S. Air Force Thunderbirds. Michelle Johnson Householder said the air show in the 1970s and '80s was one of her favorite festival events.

"It wasn't out on the beach like the later days," she said. "It was actually at the air force base. And they had huge planes. We would go out there and tour inside those planes and everything, and they would have a big grandstand for you to sit [on] and watch the air show. And they would do all their stunts right in front of you, right there on the base."

A Charleston newspaper article dated June 5, 1981, said 250,000 people were expected to attend Sun Fun that year. Another article in the May 31, 1985 issue of the *Charleston Post and Courier* said that "at least 275,000 people are expected to visit the Myrtle Beach area" for the festival. The article also mentioned a Sun Fun Mackerel Tournament that was "expected to draw more than 2,000 fishermen and 200 to 300 boats. About half the fishermen will be from out of state, with representatives from as far away as Texas. The event could bring in at least $750,000."

Sixty Years and Done

Starting in 2008, festival events were moved from downtown Myrtle Beach to the Market Common, a 114-acre shopping/dining/residential area that opened in 2008 on the site of the former Myrtle Beach Air Force Base. In the final two years of the festival, the Myrtle Beach Area Chamber of Commerce changed the parade to be a Memorial Day parade on Memorial Day weekend in May, which is a week or two earlier than the traditional Sun Fun Parade. This is why the grand marshals changed to be military-oriented, and they were Colonel Buzz Aldrin in 2010 and U.S. senator John McCain in 2011.

In 2010 and 2011, Sun Fun Festival events were shortened from the traditional four days over the first full weekend in June to two days.

The sixtieth annual Sun Fun Festival in 2011 was the last, although no one knew it at the time. Memorial Day weekend events were May 27 and 28. On the twenty-seventh, events were in downtown Myrtle Beach with the parade, Disney and Nickelodeon actor meet-and-greets, live music and parachute jumps by the Golden Knights and Team Bowman. The Miss Sun Fun USA and Miss Sun Fun Teen USA pageant was held on the twenty-eighth at the Academy of Arts, Science and Technology, a local high school.

The final events of 2011 were held June 3–5 at Grand Park at the Market Common. Wake board and personal watercraft demonstrations took place on a small lake, and the H2X Racing APBA National Jet Ski Championships were at the beachfront near Springmaid Beach. Hot cars converged for the "First Annual Sun Fun Myrtle Beach Convertible Car Show," and a couple of celebrity cars were on display: the General Lee from *Dukes of Hazzard* and the Munsters' Coffin Car.

Many vendors were on site selling food and arts and crafts, and fireworks ended the festival on Saturday night. Throughout the weekend, bands performed, and on Sunday, the final event of the sixty-year-long Sun Fun Festival was a boiled peanut–eating contest sponsored by McCall Farms of Effingham, South Carolina.

In 2012, after four years of transitioning the event from early June to Memorial Day weekend and from downtown Myrtle Beach to the Market Common, the Myrtle Beach Area Chamber of Commerce canceled the Sun Fun Festival with two months' notice and without discussion with or advance warning to Myrtle Beach mayor John Rhodes. On the day Richard Singleton, chairman of the board at the MBACC, sent a press release in April 2012 to announce the festival's suspension, the mayor said to local television station WBTW that he was, "unaware of [the] announcement, and [he planned] to get more information from the MBACC board of directors before making a comment."

The chamber's press release said:

> The MBACC board of directors has made the decision to suspend certain events this year that are not self-sustaining. With the interests of both the membership and organization in mind, the board of directors has decided that the general events held in-market in 2012 that are not self-sustained by sponsorships, ticket sales or event-specific revenue, should be suspended so our out-of-market advertising investment can be maximized and we can invest in real estate promotion.

Singleton also said in the statement that perhaps the Sun Fun Festival would return in 2013, but it did not. There were no plans for one in 2014.

The festival was conceived as a way for the chamber to bring additional tourists to Myrtle Beach, which benefitted its members. It was not meant to be a moneymaker for the chamber itself. The chamber is a nonprofit 501(c)(6) organization that reaped at least $70 million from 2009 to 2013 from a new local "penny tax" to use for promoting Myrtle Beach, which was approved by city council members without a voter referendum. Chamber president Brad Dean earned more than $350,000 in 2012.

"How in the world can someone cancel a Sun Fun because it doesn't make money?" asked Myrtle Beach architect Joel Carter in December 2013. "I don't support canceling Sun Fun. Is its purpose to draw visitors in, or is its purpose to make money? Are they supporting it so the whole community makes money, or are they supporting it so the sponsoring organization makes money?"

It would be hard to find Myrtle Beach–area locals who are happy the Sun Fun Festival was unceremoniously canceled.

Kathleen Futrell says when she heard the news she "was very disappointed. I guess the beach got so big, and [there were] so many things to do. Had they kept it up, I think it was a big drawing point, and I think it's a shame it is gone. I know it dropped from the several days it was, just to like a weekend; then it wasn't long before it just didn't get the support it had."

However, Futrell said, "People voted for Sun Fun as the best event at the beach even though it didn't exist any more."

It's true. Two years after the last Sun Fun Festival was held in 2011, it was voted by readers as a finalist for favorite event/festival in the *Sun News*'s 2013 Best of the Beach awards.

Michelle Johnson Householder feels let down:

It makes me—I hate it…Whenever I vote for people to be in office, I vote for somebody that I would hope would want to keep traditions and make new traditions. Not necessarily get rid of the old traditions. That was such a huge event. I mean, we had Sun Fun banners on every light pole going down Kings Highway for Sun Fun Week…They had those big yellow flags with a big smiley face on them. They were just awesome. And just so much to do, that whole week was…between the air show and the parade and the beauty contests and things like that out there and the bands played, all the games—tons of games—all kinds of stuff. It was just so much fun. And the whole community—everybody—you'd see everybody out there on that boulevard. Saturday morning or out there on Main Street, everybody that you knew would come out for that parade. All the locals came. And the tourists—we were totally mixed. It wasn't the same after they moved that parade over to Market Common…Why'd they have to do that?

12

MILITARY PRESENCE

In 1940, the Works Progress Administration used $112,000 from the Civil Aeronautics Administration to make the Myrtle Beach Municipal Airport capable of handling defense tasks. The Myrtle Beach mayor at the time, Benjamin Graham, "was credited with making the War Department aware of the suitability of the area for a bombing and gunnery range," according to a display at the Horry County Museum.

The 2009 Horry County Historic Resources Survey says the next step toward militarization in 1940 was when "the federal government acquired about 100,000 acres from 300 landowners to create a bombing range between the Intracoastal Waterway and Highway 90...The army also used the [newly improved] airport, and the constant flux with incoming and outgoing soldiers swelled the town's population far above its 1,600 residents in 1941." It was called the Myrtle Beach General Bombing and Gunnery Range.

The army air corps first used it. The corps mapped and photographed the area and then conducted firing practice along the oceanfront. That it could do this is an illustration of how sparsely populated the Myrtle Beach coast was at the time. Many units trained there in 1941 before going overseas for a total of "552 combat teams and 1,082 replacement crewmembers," and "more than 4,451 firing and bombing missions had been completed." Famous trainees included some who participated in the Doolittle Raid over Tokyo on April 18, 1942, with Lieutenant Colonel James Doolittle. Farrow Parkway at the former air base is named for one of those raiders: Lieutenant William G. Farrow. A Darlington native, he was captured on April 18, 1942,

Many units trained in Myrtle Beach before going overseas during World War II. *Horry County Museum, Conway, South Carolina.*

by the Japanese and executed by firing squad on October 15, 1942, at age twenty-four.

The base expanded during World War II with the addition of roads and more than one hundred buildings, including a thirty-bed hospital, a service club, a library and a bowling alley, and during the war, the buildings were camouflaged. In 1943, the base was given a new name: Myrtle Beach Army Air Field.

Genevieve "Sister" Peterkin (1928–2011) was in high school and college during World War II, and she wrote about coastal residents having blackout curtains and seeing ships burning offshore that were torpedoed by German submarines. She attended high school in Myrtle Beach, where "they let us spend our study halls as lookouts in a tower on the beach. I learned all the shapes of the German planes and the Japanese planes and, of course, the American planes, and thank goodness we never saw a plane that wasn't ours."

A prisoner of war camp opened in 1944 and, for about two years, housed some six hundred Germans. It was first located at Cane Patch Swash between present-day Seventy-first and Seventy-ninth Avenues North. "German prisoners of war were brought to a temporary camp site along the creek early in 1944," Blanche Floyd wrote in May 1993. "The site stretched from the highway to the beach, through native trees and bushes, with no houses or businesses around. The camp moved to the air base after barracks were built, with the help of the prisoners."

"Many of the prisoners were pilots captured in North Africa," a history note in the December 11, 1999 issue of the *Sun News* says. "They worked at cutting pulp wood, constructing barracks and working at various jobs at the military base." The prisoners received wages of eighty cents per day plus ten cents per day toward buying items at the base canteen, and the Horry County Museum display includes one of the wood footlockers the POWs were required to make for themselves in the base woodworking shop. Prisoner labor was also used to help repair bridges washed out in 1945 after the Great Pee Dee River flooded.

Of the six hundred or so prisoners, two died in Myrtle Beach. "One drowned swimming in the ocean," Rick Simmons wrote in the October 2013 issue of *Grand Strand Magazine*, and he is buried in Ocean Woods Cemetery. Another "committed suicide at the end of the war after learning that Germany had been defeated."

American servicemen also died in the Myrtle Beach area during World War II. Sister Peterkin recalled in her book that she was watching pilots practice firing formations while they flew A-26s and B-25s over Murrells Inlet:

> One afternoon three of these were circling to reform, and as they did the wing of one knocked the tail off another which started spiraling down. This was horrible to watch, especially because the tail gunner had escaped and opened his parachute. But the parachute caught in the pieces of the tail, so he fell as well. All that flapping white silk got snatched out of the blue sky, and the tail gunner went straight down and head first.

Peterkin screamed for her mother, who drove her to the boat company headquarters so she could alert the airmen's superiors. "The plane had fallen in the marsh and was burning. When they got there the two boys in front were trying to break the glass of the canopy and get out. The tail gunner with the parachute had died from the fall, but those two were still alive. But because of the boggy mud and the marsh the crash boat crew couldn't reach them in time. Both died."

After World War II ended, in 1945 and '46, the Myrtle Beach Army Air Field was used by military organizations like the National Guard for training. It was deactivated in October 1947, and the airport runways and tower were returned to Myrtle Beach so the municipal airport could reopen.

City officials missed the economic boost military personnel brought to Myrtle Beach businesses as well as the base's civilian employment opportunities. In 1954, plans were started to reactivate the almost four-thousand-acre base, and for the next thirty-nine years, its location near the oceanfront was a coveted assignment for airmen. Myrtle Beach was home base to 727th Aircraft Control and Warning Squadron, the 443rd Air Base Squadron and the 342nd Fighter-Day Wing, which, in 1958, was "re-designated the 354th Tactical Fighter Wing and given a fighter-bomber mission." The wing had a wartime deployment to Korat Royal Air Force Base in Thailand and was deployed during Operation Desert Shield to Southwest Asia. Squadrons were also deployed to Europe, and the base contributed its services in several overseas countries.

Having an air force base near a tourist area was not without risk. On August 18, 1958, four people were killed when a jet's engine failed at an altitude of about three hundred feet during a ground-controlled landing. The two pilots, who were injured but lived, were able to guide the aircraft away from Myrtle Beach's more densely populated areas, but it hit Springmaid Pier. The jet "struck a concession building on the fishing pier, then cartwheeled into a row of parked cars," an article in the *Logansport Press* said. The concession owner and three members of a family from New Albany, Indiana, were killed.

Other times having an air force squadron was handy, such as in July 1971, when three men were in the ocean on a disabled boat for more than two hours. Crew members of the Forty-fourth Aerospace Rescue and Recovery Squadron received a call at midnight from police looking for help, and eighteen minutes later, they had a helicopter in the air. After twenty minutes, they spotted the men, who were a mile from shore and drifting out to sea. One man was hoisted onto the helicopter while boats picked up the other two.

The base was its own little town, Ed and Joyce Herian recall. "They had the NCO club out there with great bands, lots of dancing," Joyce said. "You could bring friends from Myrtle Beach out there as long as you were a member. They had great food to eat and a big dance floor. They also had an officer's club that did the same thing, but you would have to be of higher ranks."

Joyce Herian's son, Jack Bourne, remembers, "They had summer camp out there every year. I remember Momma would enroll us in that for so many weeks. Military and civilians ran it. We'd do arts and crafts, make a potholder. I remember getting my Red Cross badge at the swimming pool out there. They had a swimming pool with two or three different diving boards; it was a really nice pool."

The same year this photo was taken at the Myrtle Beach Air Force Base in 1958, the 342nd Fighter-Day Wing became the 354th Tactical Fighter Wing. *Author's collection.*

A 1990 article in the *New York Times* revealed several U.S. Air Force bases misspent funding, including the one at Myrtle Beach: "At Myrtle Beach Air Force Base in South Carolina, $119,645 was improperly spent to buy lobster pots, crab traps, bicycles, swim fins, snorkels and badminton sets." In 1993, the base was deactivated, one of many U.S. Air Force bases closed in the same era as the military was downsized. For the local economy, it meant "the loss of nearly 5,100 jobs; as many as 1,500 homes dumped on the resale market; a 15 percent drop in students attending local schools; unemployment rates topping 20 percent; and an economic loss topping $91 million from payrolls, taxes and other revenues," a March 2013 *Sun News* article by David Wren says.

Once again, the airport was given back to Myrtle Beach.

The city wanted the former air base redeveloped and formed the Myrtle Beach Air Base Redevelopment Authority. Officers' quarters were turned into a residential community called Seagate Village, and new residential neighborhoods have been built. Many of its base buildings now house restaurants, insurance offices, a Veteran's Administration clinic, an American Red Cross office and other companies, while some buildings were torn down to make way for new amenities, like a lake and surrounding park. In 2008, a large portion was converted to become the Market Common, a live/work community with shopping, dining, a movie theater, apartments, townhomes, houses and parks. Horry Georgetown Technical College has several buildings

The guard station and gate, shown here circa 1960, remained visible to passersby on U.S. 17 for several years after the U.S. Air Force Base was deactivated in 1993. *Horry County Museum, Conway, South Carolina.*

at the former air base, including a Healthcare Education Center opened in 2012 that offers several degree programs. Soon the campus will also have a new state-of-the-art culinary arts technology building. The City of Myrtle Beach has built several sports fields near a city-run gymnasium, which are close to the Market Common and the HGTC campus.

Following the base's 1947 deactivation and reopening in the mid-1950s, much of the original base's buildings were demolished. Four are located at the Meher Baba Spiritual Center and are used as cabins, the 2009 Horry County Historic Resources Survey says. Its golf course, now operated by the city as Whispering Pines, is a remnant of the original base, but in early 2014, Myrtle Beach "city leaders say the course is a losing proposition and, if some changes aren't made, the city may have no choice but to shut it down," *My Horry News* reported.

The 2009 survey details how:

> *Either removed or demolished, buildings associated with this early military base no longer mark the location. When built, the Myrtle Beach Air Force Base included 114 buildings, runways, a secondary road system, and a bombing and gunnery range. The active base was largely to the east of the runway, with a few buildings to the west. Meanwhile, the World War II– era buildings, utilities, and portions of taxiways, among other things, were*

148

removed or demolished…On roads accessible during the survey, only the golf course and a concrete block utility building remain from the World War II–era Air Force Base. Approximately 41 structures are included in the survey from the ca. 1956 Air Force Base to the west of the runway. Many structures have already been demolished as the Myrtle Beach Air Force Base Redevelopment Authority alters the landscape to better accommodate development into a commercial and residential area…This is a unique landscape, as not many civilians have the opportunity to live on, work at, or shop at a reinvented military base. It would have been a unique and exciting marketing opportunity to keep the atmosphere of the base and to use it as a recurring theme for the site's development. With many new subdivisions and commercial strips attempting to brand themselves with memorable names or logos, the former base had a built-in theme and system of easily adaptable buildings.

In 2014, 150 historic markers dot the former base. Warbird Park, near the former base's front gate at Kings Highway, is a monument to the 354th Tactical Fighter Wing. Planes on display at the park include an A-10 Thunderbird, an A-7D Corsair and an F-100D/F Super Sabre. The park has a Wall of Service composed of granite nameplates, and the Myrtle Beach local government website says, "Everyone who served honorably at the Myrtle Beach Air Force Base, whether military or civilian, is eligible to be recognized with an engraved granite nameplate…for a $20 donation."

Within the Market Common is Valor Memorial Garden, a one-block park with sidewalks, plants, a pergola, a fountain and a grassy area where festivals and other special events are held. The city's Crabtree Memorial Gymnasium located on the former base is named for Clement Gurley Crabtree, the former recreation director of the Myrtle Beach Air Force Base, and the gym has a military museum. Myrtle Beach has a Memorial Day parade, and the entire month of May is full of city-sponsored military-oriented events.

13

OCEAN VIEW MEMORIAL HOSPITAL

B y 1949, as the permanent population of Myrtle Beach swelled and increasing numbers of tourists visited each year, the need for a hospital closer than the one in Conway became obvious. Ocean View Memorial Hospital was chartered that year, but it wasn't open for business until 1958.

Credit for conceiving the idea of a hospital in Myrtle Beach was given to Brigadier General H.B. Springs, according to a 1963 article by Jack Bass. A committee was appointed to investigate the project, and it initially sought federal, state and county government funding. However, Bass wrote, "Early leaders in the movement were advised Myrtle Beach was not yet ready for a hospital and that other areas had priority over available funds." Undeterred, the committee asked the community to help raise funds for a hospital, and civic clubs, church groups and individuals pitched in. Their determination resulted in construction of the hospital with some "$350,000 raised through individual donations and subscriptions. Five acres of land was donated as a site by Myrtle Beach Farms." The site was off Ocean Boulevard at Seventy-seventh Avenue North.

During those nine years, many fundraisers were held to benefit the hospital. The Sun Fun Festival got its start in 1951 as a way of raising money for the hospital, and locals remember that if they didn't wear beach attire to the festival, they were put in the Sun Fun jail until a fine was paid, which went to the hospital fund.

Four months before the fifty-bed hospital opened on July 2, 1958, its Women's Auxiliary had a fundraising cookbook published called *Coastal*

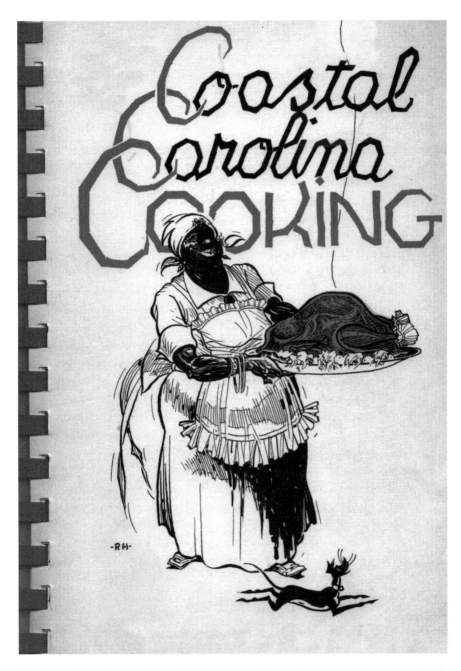

The Ocean View Memorial Hospital Women's Auxiliary sold seventeen thousand copies of this fundraising cookbook published in 1958. *Author's collection.*

Carolina Cooking, and it sold seventeen thousand copies. Its cover depicts an extremely rotund African American woman in a long dress, frilly apron and headscarf holding a platter on which rests a roast turkey, complete with paper crowns on its legs. The cookbook's editor, Mrs. C. Huston Miller, acknowledged, "Mr. Russell Henderson [is] the celebrated artist who so fittingly designed the cover."

The foreword, printed in the book in the author's own handwriting, was written by Dr. Archibald Rutledge (1883–1973), the 1934–73 South Carolina poet laureate who lived at Hampton Plantation south of Georgetown:

> *The health, the happiness, and the general welfare of any community depend very largely on the medical facilities available to it. If all these beneficent facilities can be centralized in a hospital, and dispensed from there, fortunate indeed is every family in the town or city that possesses such a medical institution. For a hospital represents Mercy and Relief in their most practical and immediately available forms. Should any one doubt the truth of this, whether or not he may have a cherished one cared for there, let him visit a hospital. There he will swiftly and poignantly learn of the universal beauty of love as he watches visitors of all classes bringing flowers and other gifts to patients looking as if anxiety and sorrow has made them more gentle and more aware of the deeply significant values of life; he will become conscious of the fact, as he watches the marvellous [sic] skill of the doctors, that the profession of medicine is the finest in the world. Was not our Master, Christ, called "The Great Physician"? He will observe with admiration the trained and affectionate proficiency of the nurses, whose tireless ministrations always mean the difference between comfort and discomfort, and at times even have the power to stay the dark hand of death itself. Surely a hospital represents all that—is best—in human nature. It is the home of compassion, the shrine of noble and tender valor. With pride and gratitude it should be revered by all. And the incessant, devoted, and mighty work of a hospital is more deserving of public recognition and support than is any other human activity known to me. A hospital is where the Good Samaritan lives.*

The hospital's first administrator was "Manson Turner, a native of Laurens, who previously served as hospital administrator in Marion. His hospital experience also includes 20 years of service with the U.S. Navy." Ocean View's founding board of directors included "President C.C. Pridgen, Treasurer P.G. Winstead, Secretary Robert H. Jones, Lee H. Kent,

Ocean View Memorial Hospital was built solely from donations, and it served the Myrtle Beach community for twenty years. *Author's collection.*

Dr. S.C. Lind, Mrs. H.B. Springs, A.P. Gandy, Mrs. Elizabeth C. Patterson, and Charles Tilghman."

The launching staff included "thirteen physicians, surgeons and other specialists," and "interest in the new Myrtle Beach Hospital is evidenced by the fact that applications have come from nurses and other prospective employees from all sections of the nation. Members of the present staff represent fifteen different states and three foreign nations."

Ocean View Memorial Hospital's first baby was born to Mrs. George Inabinet of Myrtle Beach, who had a daughter, Mary Catherine. In 1963, the hospital celebrated five years of operation with a birthday party attended by five-year-old Mary Catherine. During those first five years, Jack Bass wrote, 1,181 babies were born and 10,386 patients were admitted.

The five-year mark was also celebrated with a new wing containing thirteen private rooms, an additional second reception area with a lobby and lounge, a conference room and a medical library. "The $110,000 addition was paid for entirely by private funds, continuing the history of the hospital of never receiving any state or federal funds. The Duke Foundation made a $30,000 grant for the new addition," Bass wrote. Each of the new private rooms had its own restroom, electric bed, telephone, intercom connection to the nurses' station and "a connection for piped oxygen." Staff had increased to include "nine active doctors, three courtesy doctors, 21 registered nurses, three licensed practical nurses, 18 auxiliary nursing personnel, a dietician, four laboratory technicians and an X-ray technician."

The hospital operated "entirely from patient fees. The hospital manages to operate in the black, without tax support, and yet accepts charity patients. All revenue in excess of expenses goes into new equipment." Board of director members in 1963 were chairman A.E. Jackson, vice-chairman R.H. Govan, secretary Mrs. C.C. Pridgen, treasurer L.N. Clark, assistant treasurer Mrs. Elizabeth Patterson and C.C. Huitt, Frank Hughes, James Dew and Judge Claude Epps.

"It was such a beautiful hospital," Joyce Herian said. Her son, Jack Bourne, who was born at Ocean View Memorial, remembers visiting the hospital: "Outside the doors it had big goldfish ponds, where you could sit and look at the koi."

In 1968, the hospital was issued a building permit for a physical therapy annex estimated to cost $56,000. "By 1970 the hospital had 96 beds and a new emergency room wing," Barbara Stokes wrote, "but community needs and growth were rapidly outpacing the hospital's capabilities."

In 1971, Michelle Johnson Householder was born at Ocean View Memorial, and she remembers when her younger sister was born there:

> *When my sister was born, my dad forgot to put shoes on me when we went to the hospital to see my sister. I was barefoot and so excited. My mom opened the back door of the hospital and let us in, because her room was right there. I remember all the sand spurs, and it was a big traumatic thing. I didn't care about my sister after that. Mom fussed at Dad because he forgot to put shoes on me.*

Only twenty years after it opened, Ocean View Memorial Hospital closed in 1978, when a new hospital, today known as Grand Strand Medical Center, was built. In 2014, it remains the only hospital in the city of Myrtle Beach.

"[The hospital site] is just a vacant lot now," Householder said. "They were having problems with people breaking in, homeless people sleeping there, so they had to tear it down."

MOTORCYCLE RALLIES

Bikers still visit the Myrtle Beach area, but not nearly as many cross the boundary into the Myrtle Beach City limits as in years past. And that's just fine with city hall.

Motorcycle enthusiasts have held rallies in the Myrtle Beach area since 1940, and the longest-running annual rally is traditionally held in mid-May. Before 2008, it was known as Myrtle Beach Bike Week or simply Harley Week. In 1980, the Flaming Knight Riders motorcycle club at the north end of the Grand Strand launched another annual rally held Memorial Day weekend. It is called Black Bike Week, or the Memorial Weekend Rally, although riders of all races participate. A third and smaller fall rally has been gaining in popularity since after the millennium.

Through the years, the two May rallies saw their attendances swell into the hundreds of thousands, and eventually the second rally outnumbered the first. Some bikers arrived early at the rallies or stayed beyond the official rally dates, which changed the tone of Myrtle Beach tourism during almost the entire month of May. The first rally was and is composed of mostly white Harley bikers ages twenty-five to sixty. The second rally has historically been mostly African American street bikers ages twenty to sixty, with a high number in the twenty to thirty-five age range. However, both rallies include people of all races and ages and don't discriminate. At the rallies, anyone on a motorcycle is just another biker.

As the rallies have grown, so has their rambunctiousness. In the 1990s and 2000s, the first May rally became notorious for activities such as "weenie bite" contests, in which women stand up on the back pegs and try to bite a hot dog on a string; increasingly suggestive clothing, including body paint instead of clothing or moments of females going topless; drag racing; tire burnouts; excessive revving; driving under the influence; fights; and other crimes. Reports in the media about biker groups such as Hells Angels coming to possibly spread mayhem made many residents uneasy.

The second May rally has its epicenter at the tiny municipality of Atlantic Beach, which is a few blocks within the city of North Myrtle Beach. Also known as the Black Pearl, it is the only beach along the Grand Strand where blacks were welcome before integration. This rally became increasingly stressful for some locals as female bikers wore thong bikinis, and riders sped and passed traffic by splitting lanes. Groups of bikers, along with thousands of people driving souped-up cars, impeded the flow of traffic. Traffic was often at a standstill on U.S. 17 and other areas during the peak Memorial Day weekend rally. The expense of three hundred additional police officers and post-rally cleanups became an increasing civic burden.

As more people attended both rallies, there were also increased numbers of motorcycle-related traffic accidents resulting in injuries and deaths.

Some locals, such as business owners, count on bikers to give a large and welcome boost to their incomes before schoolchildren are on summer breaks. A significant number of locals dread the traffic congestion, noise and increased amount of crimes during bike weeks, but they accept it as part of living in a tourist area. Other locals became fed up with the May rallies, saying they were sick of all the noise and traffic.

As the number of bikers swelled, an increasing number of Myrtle Beach city residents complained to their elected city officials and asked them to do something about it. Mark McBride was mayor of Myrtle Beach from 1998 through 2006, and he made public comments about not liking the clothing and actions, which he considered obscene, at bike rallies. In 1999, he asked the South Carolina governor to send in the National Guard to keep order, but the governor, Jim Hodges, declined.

Controversy over the bike rallies continued to build. The NAACP started to monitor the rallies for instances of discrimination, and several times, it made accusations or filed charges against business owners for closing their businesses or discouraging service. Lawsuits were also filed against the City of Myrtle Beach for perceived discrimination in how the two May rallies were handled. The city responded by creating a one-way traffic chute on Ocean Boulevard and closing off many streets during both rallies.

Tensions reached crescendos in 2008 and 2009. In May 2008, during the second rally, a local twenty-year-old college student was shot and killed by a local teenager during a dispute over a parking spot. In September 2008, the Myrtle Beach City Council passed fifteen new ordinances that declared "unpermitted events and rallies to be public nuisances" and restricted the hours of operation for businesses that serve beer and wine and allow "drinking contests or games, or contests involving disrobing, or 'wet t-shirt', 'Girls Gone Wild' or similar contests." One ordinance prohibited businesses from permitting alcohol consumption in parking lots, which was a blow to many venues that erected tents in parking lots to serve beer and food during bike rallies, and for bikers who brought lawn chairs and sat in the parking lots of their Ocean Boulevard hotels to watch motorcycles parade by.

Ordinance 2008-68 addressed vehicles' allowed sound level and said:

> *It shall be an administrative infraction and a public nuisance to operate within the city limits a motorcycle manufactured before December 31, 1982, or any custom built motorcycle manufactured before December 31, 1982, that is not equipped with an unmodified exhaust muffler bearing the Federal EPA required labeling compliance applicable to the motorcycle's model year" and "racing or revving of engines by manipulation of the accelerator, gas pedal, or carburetor in applying fuel to the engine in a greater amount than is necessary whether the vehicle is either in motion or standing still.*

The new ordinance that caused the most outrage was No. 2008-64, which required anyone riding a motorcycle within the city limits to wear helmets and protective eyewear. It also set requirements for what types of helmets could be worn and mandated the helmets had to have a certain type of safety sticker on them. It is legal for adults to ride motorcycles without helmets in the state of South Carolina.

Tom Rice, a Myrtle Beach tax attorney who went on to become Horry County Council chairman and then a United States Congress member, supported an anti-bike rally group and website called Take Back May, which was a significant impetus in curtailing the motorcycle rallies. In June 2009, the Take Back May members, made up of local residents and business owners, held a lunch to celebrate their successful anti-biker campaign at the Myrtle Beach train depot. A few dozen bikers also showed up to protest the celebration.

Most motorcycle riders—locals and those who always visit during one of the rallies—and many business owners who counted on bike rally income

In 2008, Myrtle Beach leaders passed an ordinance mandating that motorcycle riders had to wear helmets within city limits. *Photo by Matt Silfer, Silver Studios.*

were outraged at the official pulling away of Myrtle Beach's welcome mat. Myrtle Beach mayor John Rhodes went even further by saying, on the city website, later recorded by the examiner.com, "Myrtle Beach is no longer the location for two long-running motorcycle events. After many years, our residents grew weary of three weeks of noise and traffic congestion each May, and they asked (the) City Council to end the events. As a result, the Harley-Davidson Dealers Association Spring Rally and the Atlantic Beach Memorial Day Bikefest will not be held in Myrtle Beach."

The Myrtle Beach Area Chamber of Commerce also weighed in against motorcycle rallies and "launched a website and brochure campaign to get the word out that motorcyclists should stay away during the rally season," according to a 2009 American Motorcyclist Association article.

In April 2009, forty-nine people who had been cited in Myrtle Beach for violating the helmet and protective eyewear ordinance filed a lawsuit protesting it, and in June 2010, the ordinance was declared invalid by the South Carolina Supreme Court "on the grounds that it is superseded by state law." The helmet law's repeal took effect immediately. Myrtle Beach mayor John Rhodes said in response that city officials still didn't support biker rallies.

In 2009, the two May motorcycle rallies were still held from May 8 to 17 and May 21 to 25, but official events were planned outside Myrtle Beach city limits, such as in Murrells Inlet and North Myrtle Beach. Biker websites and other information sources pledged to never spend any more money in Myrtle Beach and used the slogan "Not a Dime in '09." Other bikers, such as those in a group called Help Eliminate Lousy Politicians, did not support the "Not a Dime in '09" movement, saying the best way to retaliate against the new ordinances was to vote elected city officials out of office instead of punishing Myrtle Beach business owners.

Myrtle Beach reinforced its anti-rally stance by setting up a traffic checkpoint on Friday, May 15, 2009, on U.S. 501 near the U.S. 17 Bypass interchange—one of the busiest main roads leading to Myrtle Beach—which resulted in "the beach-bound traffic lanes backed up for much of the late morning," a local media television station reported. People stuck in traffic, as well as local business owners, were angry. The article quotes one businessman as saying, "It's actually a black eye for the city. I don't know who could've looked at that or thought about this and said, 'Gee, this is a good idea.'" City officials thought it was a good idea. "Myrtle Beach spokesman Mark Kruea said it was not a coincident [*sic*] this checkpoint was set up when and where it was."

Many bikers attended meetings in 2009 to protest and discuss the way Myrtle Beach leaders treated them during rallies. *Photo by Becky Billingsley.*

Many people were incensed that motorcycle rally events were eliminated in Myrtle Beach as the United States was in the depths of the great recession. Those feelings burst into flames when, on May 26, 2009, Myrtle Beach council members voted to implement a Tourism Development Fee, which is an additional one-cent sales tax on most items purchased within the city of Myrtle Beach. For some bikers, the penny tax reinforced the belief that city officials want to encourage selective tourism by trying to lure specific types of visitors who are not bikers.

"The chamber has received nearly $69.5 million from the local-option sales tax since its inception to pay for advertisements that promote Myrtle Beach to out-of-state visitors," says an article written by *Sun News* reporter

David Wren published on August 26, 2013. Eighty percent of the tax goes to the Myrtle Beach Area Chamber of Commerce for "out of market tourism promotion" while the other 20 percent is used to lower property tax bills for Myrtle Beach residents. The passage of the tax by council members without putting it to a public vote has been a matter of debate ever since with admissions that some council members and other politicians, some on the state level, were given envelopes containing checks totaling $324,500 by chamber representatives. Many locals think the campaign donations were payments for passing the penny tax.

"An Internal Revenue Service agent has confirmed that a federal criminal investigation into political donations linked to the Myrtle Beach Area Chamber of Commerce is continuing," Wren wrote in the August 2013 article. "The joint investigation with the FBI is now in its third year."

Horry County also took action to curtail bike rally events. In 2008, the county issued six hundred permits for May bike rallies, and in 2009, that number was reduced to four hundred, Thema Ponton of WBTW News 13 reported in March 2009.

On May 22, 2011, following the first spring rally, *Sun News* reporter Tonya Root wrote, "Vendors, visitors and residents said this year's rally increased in size and attendance, but it was not close to the rally's heyday of several years ago when as many as 500,000 people attended. They estimated between 75,000 and 100,000 people were in town for this year's rally."

In 2012, the Horry County Council, led by chairman Tom Rice, discussed limiting or revoking bike rally vendor licenses throughout the county during May biker rallies. "Out of the discussion came a third option of reducing the permits to only three days. Council chairman Tom Rice backed that option, but he also is weighing the option of throwing out permits all together," says a February 14, 2012 article by Ryan Naquin of News Channel 15 in Myrtle Beach. Naquin quotes Rice as saying, "I would prefer to see the rallies be shortened and/or the permits eliminated all together."

The council voted in April 2012 to leave the permit time length at seven days. However, the number of vendor permit applications dwindled. In April 2013, Lauren Hinnant of WBTW reported the number of Horry County biker rally vendor permits issued in 2012 was sixty-five. Three weeks before the 2013 rallies began, Hinnant reported, fifty-one permits had been sold at a cost of $800 each.

After the 2013 fall bike rally, biker columnist Eric Rutherford wrote in *Weekly Surge* that "after years of economic difficulties and the damage done by Myrtle Beach city officials, it is great to finally see the rallies gradually making a comeback. Hopefully there will be even better news to report at the spring rally."

For the 2014 spring rallies, scheduled for May 9–18 and May 23–26, a total of four hundred vendor permits in six zones were available for issue in Horry County. The first May rally vendor permits were good for seven days, the Memorial Day weekend rally permits were issued for four days and the 2014 fall rally permits were valid for seven days. The City of Myrtle Beach did not have official events scheduled for the 2014 May rallies, but it did have the entire month of May scheduled for Military Appreciation Days.

For many bikers, actions by public officials since 2008 changed the tone and appeal of the rallies, at least within the city of Myrtle Beach. These days the rallies' main activity hubs are located north, west and south of the Myrtle Beach City limits, although some Myrtle Beach businesses book entertainment during rally dates. Many bikers also now refuse to refer to the rally as Myrtle Beach Bike Week, as it was called before 2008. Some now call it the Cruisin' the Coast rally, while others simply say Spring Bike Week.

15

PRESERVING HISTORY

E nsuring more Myrtle Beach historic places and events are not lost starts with one action: speaking up.

The city of Myrtle Beach does not currently have a historic preservation committee or any historic preservation ordinances that might have helped save the Myrtle Beach Pavilion, the Ocean Forest Hotel, the Chesterfield Inn and other historic properties. The people and entities that owned them made financial decisions to remove them, and there is nothing to prevent it from happening again from a historic preservation viewpoint. Even its spot on the National Register of Historic Places did not help save the Chesterfield Inn when its owner decided to put a mini golf course in its place because there are no local ordinances to ensure properties on the NRHP are protected from demolition.

City of Myrtle Beach Planning director Jack Walker said the reason the city does not have a historic preservation board or any historic preservation ordinances is because city council members and the city manager have not made them priorities. In March 2014, Walker said:

> We don't have anything that actually gets to specific regulations dealing with historic properties. We don't really have bragging rights when it comes to historic preservation…It's got to be something that our city manager and city council want to see happen, and they say [to city planners], "All right, for the next month, your priority will be to organize and lay out the ground rules, set up some bylaws, set up what the organizational

The Chesterfield Inn, which was on the National Register of Historic Places, was razed in 2012 and replaced with this miniature golf course. *Author's collection.*

structure would be and bring back a recommendation to council." If we did that without that kind of direction from them, we would be challenged for not addressing goals that they've established for us. We work for the city manager, and he serves the city council.

"We're such a young city," Walker said. "When the planning department was created, the city wasn't even fifty years old at that point. The city then and now has always been caught up in change, wanting to be bigger and improve and compete in this aggressive, competitive tourism economy. And it has had a hard time listening to the voices of the people who say we need to save some things."

Joel Carter is a Myrtle Beach architect who is one of the charter members of the Horry County Board of Architectural Review, an organization founded in 1987 that has surveyed and documented an inventory of almost three thousand historic properties throughout the county. Hundreds of them are in Myrtle Beach. They include private homes and outbuildings, stores, theaters, cemeteries, tobacco barns, tenant houses, apartment buildings, churches, schools, bridges, boat landings, natural areas and trees. Some of them meet

As of the spring of 2014, most of the former Myrtle Beach Pavilion site is an empty lot. *Photo by Becky Billingsley.*

criteria for being listed on the NRHP—a primary consideration is that they're at least fifty years old—while many others are almost old enough.

Despite its existence, Carter says even the HCARB has little say in ensuring historic structures remain intact. "When it came right down to letting us operate like it was supposed to be operated, [Horry County Council] would not agree to it," Carter said. "They felt like it was nice to say 'We're doing something about history' as long as it was on a volunteer basis, as long as someone said, 'I want to protect my historic home or site or structure.'"

But even if the HCARB had the backing of county regulations to give its recommendations the power to save properties, it wouldn't help historic structures within the city of Myrtle Beach, Joel Carter said in December 2013:

> *If* [an Horry County] *review board* [had been] *in place in the 1970s, the Ocean Forest still would have been torn down. It's because the city of Myrtle Beach does not have…a historic preservation board.* [It] *still* [does] *not. The only thing that protects historic buildings locally is if you have a historic board that is empowered to protect them. The city or*

the county writes an ordinance, an overlay district. In order to do something to this historic building, you need to take another step and have it reviewed by that board as far as the appropriateness of the additions or renovations so it was in keeping with what was there. That's been very difficult in this area because of the personal property rights. Property rights reign supreme in South Carolina, and they are ultimately supreme in Horry County.

People who own historic properties may have concerns over being able to have control over them. Some owners think if their properties are listed on the National Register of Historic Places, they'll lose any say-so over their upkeep and ultimate fates, which isn't true. Local ordinances can pick and choose what to address for historic properties, such as keeping external ornamentation intact or ensuring that building additions have the same styles as the original structures. Carter said:

There are several people with historic properties who did not want the interference of a board telling them what they could do with it or stipulating certain conditions under which they could either tear it down or move it or add on to it. It's kind of like too much government interference, and that makes sense in a lot of ways. Although, zoning does that all the time…Most of the time with local ordinances, they don't care anything you do inside of [the building] *unless it has a monumental stair or signature element of that building or site. But if you maintain the appearance of it, you can even add on to a historic building, as long as you don't destroy the fabric that's there that could be taken off later.*

What placement on the National Register of Historic Properties can achieve is protection of the site in the event a federal project, such as a highway, is planned there. There is "no protection whatsoever unless federal funds are involved in that project," Carter said. If no federal funds are involved and there are no local ordinances to protect the structure, then the owner can choose to demolish it.

Local historic preservation ordinances "don't have to be at the Charleston level or Philadelphia or Washington, D.C.," Carter said. Some people worry that properties officially designated as historic will be restricted regarding what color a building may be painted or being told they can't put vinyl siding on it, but "there are actually districts where vinyl siding is allowed. As long as that vinyl siding matches the shape, the profile, the pattern and does not destroy the historic elements of the time, it can be allowed. Still, people

Myrtle Beach's unique Flatiron Building, which was on its own island, was replaced by Nance Plaza. *Barbara Horner collection.*

feel very, very strongly about that. They don't know it's possible in some districts…local ordinances can modify national standards. It doesn't have to be national park standards. It can be less than that but enough to protect it."

When citizens have spoken up to ask for help from Myrtle Beach City Council to preserve specific historic structures, its members have responded positively. The circa 1937 Myrtle Beach train depot was slated to be demolished by its owner, but after a public outcry, the city purchased the building and land in 1999 for $750,000. The city formed the Myrtle Beach All Aboard Committee, a volunteer group that raised more than $650,000 to improve the site and get it listed on the NRHP. It reopened in 2004 as a "public facility for meetings, committees, receptions, activities and parties," according to city literature about the site. "The city operates the building and makes it available to groups for a nominal fee. Everyone who enters the great hall, with its exposed wood trusses, plank flooring, brick walls and sliding freight doors, is reminded of the glory days of train travel."

The circa 1932 Myrtle Beach Colored School was the first public school in the Myrtle Beach area for African American students. It was in the path of a 2001 road-widening project, and a group of former students asked city council members to help save it. The council provided $40,000 to get the former students started on the process but city literature says, "The building was beyond repair and had to be dismantled in July 2001. On July 1, 2004, City Council set aside $250,000 toward construction. On March 8, 2005, Burroughs & Chapin donated a parcel of land. Centex

Homes quickly stepped up with a promise of construction materials and workers to rebuild the old school. Horry County Schools donated $120,000 to the effort with a plan to open their adult education program in the building." The school, which essentially is a replica of the original structure, opened in 2006 as the Historic Myrtle Beach Colored School Museum and Education Center.

Pine Lakes Inn, today known as Pine Lakes Country Club, was originally supposed to be part of a luxurious seaside resort called Arcady. *Author's collection.*

Pine Lakes Country Club, which was formerly the Ocean Forest Hotel and Country Club that was part of the Woodside brothers' plan for a luxurious seaside community called Arcady, opened in 1927. Known affectionately as "the Grandaddy," it had the Myrtle Beach area's first golf course, and it is still operating. In 1996, it was listed on the NRHP, and in 2009, the building was restored to gorgeous splendor.

More than a dozen pocket parks around Myrtle Beach commemorate notable people in the city's history, like Bathsheba Bowens Memorial Park, which preserves the memory of a young woman who died at age sixteen and "lived a beautiful and useful life that is an example to all young people to follow," city literature says. Chapin Park is named for Simeon Brooks Chapin, who worked for and donated extensively to local philanthropic projects. Chapin Park used to have a wading pool, where children splashed and played with toy boats. In modern times, it is known as a place where homeless people spend a lot of time, and the City of Myrtle Beach passed ordinances prohibiting people from giving them food while at the park.

Brigadier General Holmes B. Springs, who was instrumental in turning Myrtle Beach into a resort area, has a 2.6-acre park named after him. Nance Plaza in the historic downtown area is named for Daniel Wayne Nance and Mary Ellen Todd Nance, who owned a farm at the south end of town and worked to develop Myrtle Beach. The Ocean Forest Hotel, Withers Swash and Spivey Beach all have parks.

Some streets are named after historic notables, such as Mr. Joe White Avenue. Julius "Joe" White shined shoes for a living and was a much beloved person to all who knew him. The city also has designated historic neighborhoods, like the predominantly African American neighborhood formerly known as Tin Top Alley. Now known as the Carrie Mae Johnson Neighborhood between Nance and White Streets, it commemorates a resident who "was known for her beautiful hats and big smile."

A neighborhood within Myrtle Beach was listed on the NRHP starting in 1998. The Myrtle Heights–Oak Park Historic District is off Ocean Boulevard between Thirty-second and Forty-sixth Avenues North, and its homes began to be constructed in the early 1930s. The South Carolina Department of Archives and History says it is "a collection of about sixty-five architecturally distinctive properties and representative building types. The majority of these oceanside residences are two-story frame buildings, many of them with one- or two-story attached garages, two-story detached garage apartments, or one-story attached servants' quarters. The most prevalent stylistic influence is Colonial Revival, but elements of the Classical Revival, Tudor Revival, and Bungalow/ Craftsman styles are also represented."

Other Myrtle Beach properties on the NRHP as of the spring of 2014 include five Rainbow Court Hotel buildings constructed between 1935 and 1959 at 405 Flagg Street, the circa 1927 Pleasant Inn at 200 Broadway Street, the Myrtle Beach Atlantic Coast Line Railroad Station near Eighth Avenue North and the Pine Lakes Country Club. Another neighborhood city planners Jack Walker and Diane Moskow-McKenzie say they would like to see placed on the NRHP and zoned with historic preservation in mind is the Withers Swash Neighborhood.

When the former Myrtle Beach Air Force Base was redeveloped, the city could not possibly save all buildings, but many are still intact. Several were repurposed for businesses, and the base hospital got a modern new façade to become a heath services education center. Warbird Park was built, some 150 historical markers were placed throughout the area and a military museum was installed at the city's Crabtree Gymnasium located at the former base.

Economic opportunities are why many historic structures are lost. When faced with the decision to spend money on upkeep for an aging motel or beach cottage or accept a developer's offer of millions of dollars for the oceanfront property, anyone would have to think hard about whether preserving history is worth it.

"We need to create a way of understanding there's value gained from preserving historic properties," Jack Walker said. "It's not just a matter of passionately wanting to save the old stuff…it's got to make business sense."

Preserving historic residential properties is more achievable than saving commercial buildings, Walker said, because zoning says, "This is a residential zone, and we won't let commercial uses come in and change the value of the land so that demolition occurs due to the marketplace." However, he says there are ways to make historic commercial buildings more financially lucrative. Owners of Populuxe motels could band together and create a Populuxe district that is appealing as a unique nostalgic vacation destination. Kings Highway is a historic corridor that could have commercial development designed to enhance the idea of history as a "network of villages where you stop, you walk, you shop, you have coffee, you enjoy the bar scene that might be in one of them. It's about creating uniqueness and character and quality that strengthen the surrounding neighborhoods, and then there's a reason for those buildings to be there instead of [more modern development]. We're trying to build the future as well as save the past."

The Beverly Motel at 703 North Ocean Boulevard was a Populuxe motel torn down in 2013. *Photo by Becky Billingsley.*

Unless additional focus is placed on historic preservation within Myrtle Beach, more structures will be lost. Several projects have been put on hold due to the economy, but when it recovers, there will be much more demolition. Some of the historic property owners have "really big plans," Walker said. "There are about thirty major high-rises that have not been built," he said.

"The land has already been assembled, and they are just hoping that the economy turns around. You'll see more of these older buildings come down when that kind of economy returns."

Diane Moskow-McKenzie said:

History is important. It really is. Maybe by continuing to remind people that we do have something important to preserve, they'll learn that. When we were doing the Harlem and Carrie Mae Johnson neighborhood projects, we met with a neighborhood committee made up of people who lived here since they were born. We kept asking them about their history, and they didn't really think they had a history. But you start talking to them one-on-one, and they start reminiscing. And they realize they do have a history and understand the need to preserve. It's almost like you have to teach people, "What you have is important."

BIBLIOGRAPHY

CHAPTER 1

Aiken Standard and Review. "From the Myrtle Beach News." September 3, 1941.

Bartram, William. *Travels Through North & South Carolina, Georgia, East & West Florida, the Cherokee Country, the Extensive Territories of the Muscogulges, or Creek Confederacy, and the Country of the Choctaws; Containing An Account of the Soil and Natural Productions of Those Regions, Together with Observations on the Manners of the Indians*. Digital edition. Chapel Hill: University of North Carolina, 2001.

Bell, Terry. "Construction Boom Reaches New Level at Grand Strand." *Florence Morning News*, September 8, 1973.

Berry, C.B. "Amid Holly and Briar, the 'Bays' Beckon Us." *Sun News*, February 11, 1995.

———. "Long Bay Was Route Before Waterway Built." *Sun News*, October 23, 1993.

———. "Maps Visual Aid in Study of History." *Sun News*, August 15, 1994.

———. "River Ferries Vital to Getting Around." *Sun News*, July 15, 1995.

———. "Roots of Todd Family Run Deep in MB Area." *Sun News*, January 20, 1996.

———. "Settlers Vacated Intended Home." *Sun News*, May 9, 1992.

———. "Singleton Swash Used to be Dunes." *Sun News*, August 7, 1993.

———. "Strand Treacherous for Early 'Tourists'." *Sun News*, April 29, 1995.

———. "Withers Families Were Early Settlers." *Sun News*, July 7, 1990.

Brockington, Lee. Personal interview. Georgetown, March 20, 2013.

Butler, Johnny. Personal interview. Myrtle Beach, November 1, 2013.

City of Myrtle Beach. "Withers Swash District Plan: Conceptual Study for an Environmental Community." 2010. http://www.cityofmyrtlebeach. com/withers.html.

Floyd, Blanche. "Grand Strand Teems with Indian History." *Sun News*, June 6, 1992.

———. "Hurl Rocks Once Called Hearl Rocks." *Sun News*, June 1, 1991.

———. "Stories Behind Strand's Names." *Sun News*, May 8, 1993.

———. "Withers Swash Once Was Clear and Clean." *Sun News*, November 9, 1991.

———. "Yaupon, Myrtle Grow Wild on the Strand." *Sun News*, January 27, 1996.

Gasque, Pratt. *Rum Gully Tales from Tuck 'Em Inn*. Orangeburg, SC: Sandlapper Publishing Co., 1990.

Joyner, Kelly Paul. "Oyster Roasts, Trips to Beach Recalled." *Sun News*, July 20, 1990.

Milliken, Helen. *From the Beginning: A History of the Burroughs & Chapin Company*. Myrtle Beach: Sheriar Press, 2004.

Mills, Robert. *Atlas of the State of South Carolina*. Horry District. Surveyed by Harlee, 1820. Improved for Mills's Atlas 1825. Map Collection. South Carolina Department of Archives and History, Columbia.

New South Associates. *Horry County Historic Resource Survey*. Stone Mountain, Georgia, June 30, 2009.

North Carolina History Project. "Venus Flytrap." 2010. http://www. northcarolinahistory.org/encyclopedia/463/entry.

Schoepf, Johann David. *Travels in the Confederation* [1783–1784]. Translated and edited by Alfred J. Morrison. Digital version. Philadelphia, PA: William J. Campbell, 1911.

Simmons, Rick. *Hidden History of the Grand Strand*. Charleston, SC: The History Press, 2010.

South Carolina Plantations. "Peter Vaught's Plantation–Myrtle Beach– Horry County." 2014. http://south-carolina-plantations.com/horry/ peter-vaughts.html.

South Carolina State Trails Program. "Historic Trail Routes." 2008. http:// www.sctrails.net/trails/misc/historic.html.

Sun News. Millennium Moment. November 18,19, 1999; December 2,11, 1999.

Vereen, Ann. Personal interview. Myrtle Beach, November 6, 2013.

Vereen, Mike. Personal interview. Myrtle Beach, December 17, 2014.

Chapter 2

Brockington, Lee. "Coastal History Full of Hurricane Stories." *Sun News*, September 22, 1990.

Butler, Johnny. Personal interview. Myrtle Beach, November 1, 2013.

Davis, Walter. "Hurricanes of 1954." *Monthly Weather Review* (December 1954). http://www.aoml.noaa.gov/hrd/hurdat/mwr_pdf/1954.pdf.

Florence Morning News. "Our Beaches." July 4, 1947.

Floyd, Blanche. "Burned Vessel Remains in MB's Sand Dunes." *Sun News*, August 3, 1991.

Futrell, Kathleen. Personal interview. Myrtle Beach, November 26, 2013.

Householder, Michelle Johnson. Personal interview. Myrtle Beach, November 14, 2013.

Milliken, Helen. *From the Beginning: A History of the Burroughs & Chapin Company*. Myrtle Beach, SC: Sheriar Press, 2004.

National Oceanic and Atmospheric Administration. "Historical Hurricane Tracks," 2014. http://csc.noaa.gov/hurricanes/#.

New South Associates. *Horry County Historic Resource Survey*. Stone Mountain, Georgia, June 30, 2009.

Smith, Marcus. "Fickle Hazel Struck Hard in Myrtle Beach." *Sun News*, October 14, 1995.

South Carolina State Climatology Office. "South Carolina Hurricane Climatology." 2014. http://www.dnr.sc.gov/climate/sco/Tropics/hurricanes_affecting_sc.php.

Stokes, Barbara. *Greetings from…Myrtle Beach: A History, 1900–1980*. Columbia: University of South Carolina Press, 2007.

Thomas, Wynness. "Cottage Defies the Fury of Hazel." *Sun News*, March 6, 1993.

Vereen, Ann. Personal interview. Myrtle Beach, November 6, 2013.

Chapter 3

Aiken Standard. "Lift Up Your Eyes." June 14, 1929.

City of Myrtle Beach Comprehensive Plan. Myrtle Beach, March 6, 2014.

Florence Morning News. "Expect Big Crowds at Myrtle Beach." June 29, 1930.

Milliken, Helen. *From the Beginning: A History of the Burroughs & Chapin Company*. Myrtle Beach, SC: Sheriar Press, 2004.

New South Associates. *Horry County Historic Resource Survey.* Stone Mountain, Georgia, June 30, 2009.

Smith, Marcus J. "Traveling to Beach Not Always Simple." *Sun News*, April 22, 1995.

Sun News. Millennium Moment. November 27, 1999; December 25, 1999.

CHAPTER 4

Aiken Standard. "Myrtle Beach Charms J.A. Dunn." May 20, 1927.

City of Myrtle Beach Comprehensive Plan. Myrtle Beach, March 6, 2014.

City of Myrtle Beach Local Government Page. "History." Myrtle Beach, South Carolina. 2010. http://www.cityofmyrtlebeach.com/didyouknow.html.

Horner, Barbara. Personal interview. Myrtle Beach, January 16, 2014.

South Carolina Department of Archives and History. "National Register Properties in South Carolina," 2014. http://www.nationalregister.sc.gov/horry/S10817726016/index.htm.

Stokes, Barbara. *Greetings from…Myrtle Beach: A History, 1900–1980.* Columbia: University of South Carolina Press, 2007.

Sun News. Millennium Moment. November 11, 1999; December 28, 1999.

CHAPTER 5

City of Myrtle Beach Comprehensive Plan. Myrtle Beach, March 6, 2014.

"Current Population Reports: Consumer Income." U.S. Department of Commerce, Bureau of the Census, Washington, D.C., April 27, 1954.

"Did You Know?" City of Myrtle Beach website, Myrtle Beach. http://www.cityofmyrtlebeach.com/didyouknow.html.

Florence Morning News. "Bakers Will Hold Meeting Myrtle Beach." June 3, 1955.

———. "Beach Permits." October 8, 1968.

Florence Morning News Review. "Governor's Ball and Formal Thanksgiving Opening." Advertisement, Myrtle Beach Sales Company. November 20, 1926.

———. "Myrtle Beach Development on Mammoth Scale." January 24, 1926.

Hardee, Lesta Sue, and Janice McDonald. *Myrtle Beach Pavilion.* Charleston, SC: Arcadia Publishing, 2010.

Horner, Barbara. Personal interview. Myrtle Beach, January 16, 2014.

Jones, Karon Bowers. Telephone interview. November 26, 2013.

Liebs, Chester. *Main Street to Miracle Mile: American Roadside Architecture*. Baltimore, MD: Johns Hopkins University Press, 1995.

Milliken, Helen. *From the Beginning: A History of the Burroughs & Chapin Company*. Myrtle Beach, SC: Sheriar Press, 2004.

News and Courier. "Myrtle Beach Landmark, Lafayette Manor, Razed." November 19, 1960.

New South Associates. *Horry County Historic Resource Survey*. Stone Mountain, Georgia, June 30, 2009.

Robesonian. "Fairmont Newsletter: Sunday School Excursion to Myrtle Beach Proposed." July 10, 1911.

————. "Season Begins at Myrtle Beach." June 3, 1935.

Semi-Weekly (Lumberton) Robesonian. "Sea Side Hotel." Advertisement. June 8, 1911.

South Carolina Department of Archives and History. "National Register Properties in South Carolina: Chesterfield Inn, Horry County, 700 N. Ocean Blvd., Myrtle Beach," 2013. http://www.nationalregister.sc.gov/horry/S10817726008/index.htm.

Spartanburg Herald-Journal. "Closing of Inn Is End of Era." July 7, 1985.

Sumter Daily Item. "Closing of Patricia Inn Will End Era." June 6, 1985.

Sun News. Millennium Moment. November 13, 1999; December 8, 1999.

CHAPTER 6

Aiken Standard. "New $1,500,000 Hotel to Open at Myrtle Beach Early in December." October 25, 1929.

Bourne, Jack. Personal interview. Murrells Inlet, January 9, 2014.

Florence Morning News Review. "Myrtle Beach Development on Mammoth Scale." January 24, 1926.

————. "Woodside Brothers Announce Big Program Myrtle Beach." June 6, 1926.

Herian, Ed. Personal interview. Murrells Inlet, January 9, 2014.

Herian, Joyce. Personal interview. Murrells Inlet, January 9, 2014.

Jones, Karon Bowers. Telephone interview. November 26, 2013.

Milliken, Helen. *From the Beginning: A History of the Burroughs & Chapin Company*. Myrtle Beach, SC: Sheriar Press, 2004.

New South Associates. *Horry County Historic Resource Survey*. Stone Mountain, Georgia, June 30, 2009.

Robesonian. "The Formal Opening Friday, May 31st for the 1935 Summer Season." Advertisement, Ocean Forest Hotel. May 30, 1935.

————. "New Yorker Wins in Myrtle Beach Contest." August 29, 1935.

Utterback, JoAnne. Personal Interview. Myrtle Beach, February 6, 2014.

Vereen, Ann. Personal interview. Myrtle Beach, November 6, 2013.

CHAPTER 7

Beacham, Frank. "This Magic Moment: When the Ku Klux Klan Tried to Kill Rhythm & Blues Music in South Carolina." *Toward the Meeting of the Waters: Currents in the Civil Rights Movement of South Carolina during the Twentieth Century*. Columbia: University of South Carolina Press, 2008.

Bell, Terry. "Construction Boom Reaches New Level at Grand Strand." *Florence Morning News*, September 8, 1973.

Carter, Horace. "Arrests Made in Klan Killing; Investigation by Sheriff Continues." *Tabor City Tribune*, September 6, 1950.

————. "Klansman Killed in Horry Gun Fight." *Tabor City Tribune*, August 30, 1950.

Florence Morning News. "Water System For Beach Announced." December 29, 1973.

Floyd, Blanche. "Chapin's Store Was Town Center." *Sun News*, August 21, 1993.

Floyd, Blanche W. "Chapin's." *Sandlapper Magazine* (Summer 2003).

Jones, Karon Bowers. Telephone interview. November 26, 2013.

McMillan, Susan Hoffer. *Myrtle Beach and Conway in Vintage Postcards*. Charleston, SC: Arcadia Publishing, 2001.

Milliken, Helen. *From the Beginning: A History of the Burroughs & Chapin Company*. Myrtle Beach, SC: Sheriar Press, 2004.

New South Associates. *Horry County Historic Resource Survey*. Stone Mountain, Georgia, June 30, 2009.

Stokes, Barbara. *Greetings from…Myrtle Beach: A History, 1900–1980*. Columbia: University of South Carolina Press, 2007.

Sun News. Millennium Moment. November 15, 16, 1999; December 6, 1999.

CHAPTER 8

Aiken Standard and Review. "Horse Race Bill May Bob Up." November 24, 1948.

————. "Myrtle Beach Opens May 30th." May 17, 1939.

Bojarski, Tim. "Ghost Tracks VIII: Myrtle Beach, S.C." *Hoof Beats Magazine*, February 11, 2014. Accessed online. http://xwebapp.ustrotting.com/absolutenm/templates/hoofbeats_blog.aspx?articleid=57706&zoneid=75.

Dunkirk Evening Observer. "Harness Racing Notes." April 30, 1940.

Florence Morning News. "Eatmon Again Postpones Action in Racing Case." July 19, 1947.

———. "The Eatmon Ruling." August 9, 1947.

———. "N.C. Doctor Makes Emergency Landing." July 1, 1958.

———. "Oxner to Hear Myrtle Beach Guessing Case." August 13, 1947.

———. "Race Track at Myrtle Beach to Open Today." June 3, 1938.

———. "Race Tracks Close." August 16, 1947.

———. "Sheriffs Meet Myrtle Beach." July 25, 1947.

———. "Washington Park Race Track." Advertisement. June 28, 1938.

———. "Washington Park Race Track." Advertisement. June 5, 1940.

Robesonian. "Washington Park Race Track." Advertisement. July 1, 1938.

Statesville Landmark. "So the Governor Won't Be There." July 3, 1947.

Stokes, Barbara F. *Greetings from…Myrtle Beach: A History, 1900–1980.* Columbia: University of South Carolina Press, 2007.

CHAPTER 9

Associated Press. "Bank Buys Park Site." *Statesville Record & Landmark,* March 3, 1977.

———. "Country Music Stars Make the Move to Myrtle Beach." *Wilmington Star-News,* November 20, 1984.

———. "Hearing begins in Suit Over Death." *Sumter Daily Item,* April 24, 1984.

———. "Reward Offered in Slayings." *High Point Enterprise,* September 29, 1976.

———. "Scientists Exhume Body of Dolphin." *Aiken Standard,* November 9, 1977.

———. "Waccamaw Pottery Rules the Beach." *Wilmington Star-News,* January 11, 1986.

Billingsley, Adam. E-mail interview. March 26, 2014.

Black, Bill. "Rare European Deer Killed at Strand's Serpent City." *Post and Courier,* March 11, 1968.

Burlington Daily Times News. "Myrtle Beach Chairlift Falls; Seven Are Hurt." April 23, 1973.

Butler, Johnny. Personal interview. Myrtle Beach, November 1, 2013.

Chapman, Frank. "Rollercoaster Connoisseurs Have Lots to Choose from in Finding Thrills A-Plenty." *Aiken Standard,* August 3, 1984.

Coles, John, and Tiedje, Mark. "South Carolina Movie Theaters: Myrtle Beach, S.C., Rivoli Theatre." 2013. http://www.scmovietheatres.com/myr_riv.html.

Dispatch. "There's Never a Dull Moment at Fort Caroline and Charles Towne." June 16, 1966.

Jones, Karon Bowers. Telephone interview. November 26, 2013.

McComb, Larry. "Will Balloon Ride Save Magic Harbor?" *News and Courier*, May 22, 1977.

Moore, Kimberly. "History Hangs in the Balance: New Rivoli Planned, While Old Rivoli Gathers Dust." *Weekly Surge*, June 12, 2008.

Post and Courier. "Hard Rock Park Grand Opening." May 29, 2008.

Santa Fe New Mexican. "Magic Turns into Big Business While Magicians Sell Secrets." March 24, 1998.

Stafford, Jeff. Turner Classic Movies. Cult Movies: "Don't Make Waves." 2014. http://www.tcm.com/this-month/article/919593%7C81457/Don-t-Make-Waves.html.

Stokes, Barbara. *Greetings from…Myrtle Beach: A History, 1900–1980*. Columbia: University of South Carolina Press, 2007.

CHAPTER 10

Associated Press. "Teen Dies in Plunge from Myrtle Beach Ferris Wheel." *Times-News*, July 21, 1991.

Bourne, Jack. Personal interview. Murrells Inlet, January 9, 2014.

Delaware County Daily Times. "Polish-American Eagles Citizens' Club Floor Show." Advertisement. December 2, 1960.

Florence Morning News. "Meeting Held by Medicals at Beach." July 18, 1930.

———. "Myrtle Beach Sales Co." Advertisement. September 2, 1926.

Florence Morning News Review. "Myrtle Beach to Entertain Babson and S.C. Bankers." June 3, 1927.

———. "New Orchestra at Myrtle Beach." August 6, 1925.

———. "Press Association Is to Meet Soon at Myrtle Beach." May 16, 1926.

Floyd, Blanche. "Park's Merry-Go-Round the Ride to Remember." *Sun News*, August 31, 1991.

Futrell, Kathleen. Personal interview. Myrtle Beach, November 26, 2013.

Griffith, Helen. "Around the Town." *Sarasota Herald-Tribune*, August 28, 1976. http://news.google.com/newspapers?nid=1755&dat=19760828&id=aCMhAAAAIBAJ&sjid=N2cEAAAAIBAJ&pg=6711,4470270.

Hagerstown Daily Mail. "Hagerstown Fair." Advertisement. September 13, 1954.

Hardee, Lesta Sue, and Janice McDonald. *Myrtle Beach Pavilion.* Charleston, SC: Arcadia Publishing, 2010.

Herian, Ed. Personal interview. Murrells Inlet, January 9, 2014.

Herian, Joyce. Personal interview. Murrells Inlet, January 9, 2014.

Horner, Barbara. Personal interview. Myrtle Beach, January 16, 2014.

McMillan, Susan Hoffer. *Myrtle Beach and Conway in Vintage Postcards.* Charleston, SC: Arcadia Publishing, 2001.

————. *Myrtle Beach and the Grand Strand.* Charleston, SC: Arcadia Publishing, 2004.

McVety, Samantha. Circus Fans of America Association. "Norma: The Great Circus Career of a Famous Performer." Lorain, Ohio, December 21, 2008. http://www.circus4youth.org/res_det.php?res_id=105.

Smith, Marcus J. "MB Locals, Tourists Welcomed Boardwalk." *Sun News,* June 29, 1991.

Stanfield, Jeff. "Aerialists Still Dare Life Despite Circus Tragedy." *Sarasota Herald-Tribune,* September 5, 1978. http://news.google.com/newspapers?nid=1755&dat=19780905&id=pwAkAAAAIBAJ&sjid=hGcEAAAAIBAJ&pg=6922,2357554.

Stokes, Barbara. *Greetings from…Myrtle Beach: A History, 1900–1980.* Columbia: University of South Carolina Press, 2007.

Sun News. Millennium Moment. December 15, 1999.

CHAPTER 11

Aiken Standard and Review. "Myrtle Beach Opens May 30th." May 17, 1939.

Aufdemorte, Holley. "Sun Fun Pageant Becoming Preliminary to Miss USA." *Business Wire* press release, Myrtle Beach Chamber of Commerce, January 11, 2005.

Bryant, Dawn. "Nixed Sun Fun Festival in Myrtle Beach Still Popular among Visitors." *Sun News,* November 4, 2013.

Carter, Joel. Personal interview. Myrtle Beach, December 5, 2013.

Charleston Gazette. "Sun Fun Festival." Advertisement. May 20, 1956.

City of Myrtle Beach Local Government Page. "Did You Know???" 2010. http://www.cityofmyrtlebeach.com/didyouknow.html.

Clardy, Harold (1927–2012). Personal interview. Myrtle Beach, March 2004.

Cornelson, Jimmy. "Fun in the Sun." *News and Courier,* June 5, 1981.

Gazette-Mail. "Myrtle Beach Has Angle For Anglers." May 22, 1960.

———. "Sports Car Event Slated at Myrtle Beach June 5." May 15, 1960.

Horner, Barbara. "Looking Back." *Sun News,* June 16, 1990; June 1, 8, 1991; May 29, 1993; May 7, 1994.

Hourigan, Richard R., III. "Welcome to South Carolina: Sex, Race, and the Rise of Tourism in Myrtle Beach." PhD diss., University of Alabama, 2009.

Householder, Michelle Johnson. Personal interview. Myrtle Beach, November 14, 2013.

Jones, Karon Bowers. Telephone interview. November 26, 2013.

Loris Sentinel. "Sun-Fun Festival Gives Complete Event Program." May 21, 1953.

Ottawa Journal. "Myrtle Beach Sun Fun Festival Movie Premier." May 27, 1967.

Parker, Jim. "Sun Fun Festival Puts Emphasis on Sports." *News and Courier,* May 31, 1985.

Reading Eagle. "Activities at Festival Are Listed." May 23, 1976.

Singleton, Richard. Press release on behalf of the Myrtle Beach Area Chamber of Commerce, April 2012.

Smith, Marcus J. "In Another Era, Sun, Fun and the Pageant." *Sun News,* May 27, 1995.

Star-News. "Big Parade Highlight of Sun Fun Festival." June 5, 1967.

Stokes, Barbara F. *Greetings from…Myrtle Beach: A History, 1900–1980.* Columbia: University of South Carolina Press, 2007.

Sun News. Millennium Moment. November 14, 1999.

U.S. Weather Bureau. *Climatological Data.* Ann Arbor, Michigan: National Atmospheric Administration, National Environmental Satellite, Data and Information Service, National Climatic Center, 1964.

Vereen, Ann. Personal interview. Myrtle Beach, November 6, 2103.

Visit! "Sun Fun Festival Suspended After 60 Years." April 18, 2012.

WBTW News 13, Myrtle Beach, South Carolina. "MBACC Board of Directors Suspends Sun Fun Festival." April 13, 2012. http://m.scnow.com/news/local/article_0282720b-ce46-5bbd-9f5f-a1f4c545f181.html?mode=jqm.

CHAPTER 12

Bourne, Jack. Personal interview. Murrells Inlet, January 9, 2014.

City of Myrtle Beach Local Government Page. "Crabtree Memorial Gymnasium." http://www.cityofmyrtlebeach.com/crabtree.html

———. "Wall of Service at Warbird Park." http://www.cityofmyrtlebeach.com/wall.html

"Culinary Arts Technology—Associate in Applied Science." Horry Georgetown Technical College, Conway, South Carolina. http://www.hgtc.edu/academics/academic_programs/Culinary_Arts.html.

Gale, Heather. "New Dental Clinic, Healthcare Education Center Opens at Horry Georgetown Technical College." *My Horry News*, June 7, 2012.

Herian, Ed. Personal interview. Murrells Inlet, January 9, 2014.

Herian, Joyce. Personal interview. Murrells Inlet, January 9, 2014.

Horry County Museum. Myrtle Beach POW Camp exhibit. Conway, South Carolina.

Logansport Press. "USAF Explains Jet Crash That Killed 3 Persons." August 20, 1958.

Perry, Charles. "Myrtle Beach Workshop Sees Talk of Closing Whispering Pines Golf Course." *My Horry News*, January 14, 2014. http://www.myhorrynews.com/news/business/article_812b50ca-7d49-11e3-8f36-001a4bcf6878.html.

Peterkin, Genevieve C., in conversation with William P. Baldwin. *Heaven Is a Beautiful Place*. Columbia: University of South Carolina Press, 2000.

Robesonian. "Rowland Man Among 3 Rescued From Ocean." July 13, 1971.

Schmitt, Eric. "Audit Says Air Force Misspent Nearly $10 Million." *New York Times*, August 6, 1990. http://www.nytimes.com/1990/08/06/us/audit-says-air-force-misspent-nearly-10-million.html.

Simmons, Rick. "History: Lost Landmarks." *Grand Strand Magazine*, October 2013.

South Carolina History Trail. "Myrtle Beach Bombing Range and Air Force Base." http://www.schistorytrail.com/property.html?i=49.

Wren, David. "Once Feared, Redevelopment of Myrtle Beach Air Force Base Has Been Resounding Success." *Sun News*, March 31, 2013. http://www.mcclatchydc.com/2013/03/31/187375/once-feared-redevelopment-of-myrtle.html.

CHAPTER 13

Bass, Jack. "Hospital Ends Five Years." *Florence Morning News*, June 28, 1963.

Bourne, Jack. Personal interview. Murrells Inlet, January 9, 2014.

Brinkman, Fred. "New Ocean View Hospital Operating on Full Schedule in 50-Bed Center." *Florence Morning News*, July 11, 1958.

Coastal Carolina Cooking. Published and compiled by the Women's Auxiliary to the Ocean View Memorial Hospital. Charleston, SC: Walker, Evans & Cogswell Co. Printers, 1958.

Florence Morning News. "Beach Permits." October 8, 1968.

Herian, Joyce. Personal interview. Murrells Inlet, January 9, 2014.

Householder, Michelle Johnson. Personal interview. Myrtle Beach, November 14, 2013.

Stokes, Barbara. *Greetings from…Myrtle Beach: A History, 1900–1980*. Columbia: University of South Carolina Press, 2007.

CHAPTER 14

Harley, Bryan. "S.C. Court Overrules Myrtle Beach Helmet Law." MotorcycleUSA.com, Medford, Oregon, June 9, 2010. http://www.motorcycle-usa.com/4/7177/Motorcycle-Article/S-C--Court-Overrules-Myrtle-Beach-Helmet-Law-.aspx.

Hinnant, Lauren. "Horry County Issues Vendor Permits for Bike Week, Only One Section Sells Out." WBTW News 13, Myrtle Beach, South Carolina, April 25, 2013. http://www.wbtw.com/story/22081673/horry-county-issues-vendor-permits-for-bike-week-only-one-section-sells-out.

Hosking, Bruce. "Myrtle Beach, S.C. Opposes Motorcycle Rallies." Examiner.com, March 31, 2009. http://www.examiner.com/article/myrtle-beach-s-c-opposes-motorcycle-rallies.

Khan, Aisha. "Checkpoint Backs Up Traffic, Frustrates Myrtle Beach Drivers." *Morning News Online*, May 16, 2009. http://www.scnow.com/news/local/article_3735bd36-387f-5b73-be4b-7299f13a42d4.html.

Ponton, Thema. "Horry County Finalizes Rally Vendor Permits." WBTW News 13, Myrtle Beach, South Carolina, March 18, 2009. http://www.wbtw.com/story/21072232/horry-county-finalizes-rally-vendor-permits.

Root, Tonya. "Myrtle Beach Bike Week Attendance Improves, But Still Far Off Old Numbers." *Sun News*, May 22, 2011. http://www.myrtlebeachonline.com/2011/05/22/2172658_bike-week-attendance-rallies-but.html.

Rutherford, Eric. "Myrtle Beach Area's Fall Bike Rally Making a Rally?" *Weekly Surge*, October 16, 2013.

Wachter, Paul. "Myrtle Beach's Separate and Unequal Biker Rallies." Legalaffairs.org, November/December 2005. http://www.legalaffairs.org/issues/November-December-2005/scene_wachter_novdec05.msp.

WMBF News. "Myrtle Beach City Council Passes 15 Ordinances to Limit Bikers." Myrtle Beach, South Carolina, September 9, 2008. http://www.wmbfnews.com/story/8980453/myrtle-beach-city-council-passes-15-ordinances-to-limit-bikers.

Wren, David. "Criminal Investigation Continues Into Myrtle Beach Chamber-related Campaign Donations." *Sun News*, August 26, 2013. http://www.myrtlebeachonline.com/2013/08/26/3670512/criminal-investigation-continues.html.

CHAPTER 15

Carter, Joel. Personal interview. Myrtle Beach, December 5, 2013.

City of Myrtle Beach Comprehensive Plan. Myrtle Beach, March 6, 2014.

Moskow-McKenzie, Diane. Personal interview. Myrtle Beach, March 5, 2014.

"Myrtle Beach Colored School." City of Myrtle Beach literature, Myrtle Beach, South Carolina, March 2014.

"Myrtle Beach Train Depot." City of Myrtle Beach literature, Myrtle Beach, South Carolina, March 2014.

Walker, Jack. Personal interview. Myrtle Beach, March 5, 2014.

INDEX

ABOUT THE AUTHOR

B ecky Billingsley, author of *A Culinary History of Myrtle Beach and the Grand Strand*, was a general features, food and restaurant reporter at the *Sun News* daily newspaper in Myrtle Beach and was the founding editor and journalist for *Coastal Carolina Dining* magazine. At both publications, she wrote about area history, such as renovations of former slave cabins at Hobcaw Barony in Georgetown, President George Washington's 1791 visit to the Grand Strand and local food history and traditions.

Since 2008, Becky has served information at MyrtleBeachRestaurantNews.com. She has written food, restaurant, travel and feature articles for many local, regional and national websites and publications including *South Carolina Living* magazine, *Produce Business* magazine, the *Charlotte Observer*, *Litchfield Style* magazine, the *Georgetown Times*, *Weekly Surge* and GetawaysforGrownups.com.

Becky lives in the Socastee area of Myrtle Beach with her husband of thirty-two years, Matt, and they have two adult sons. They enjoy bird-watching, boating, visiting historic sites and trying new foods.